Greece in the 1940s

A Bibliographic Companion

The MODERN GREEK STUDIES ASSOCIATION, a nonprofit organization established in 1968, is devoted to the study of the language, literature, history, institutions, and arts of modern Greece, primarily in the United States and Canada. It sponsors symposia, seminars, and publications and serves as a center for information on programs and scholarly activities in the fields of Byzantine and modern Greek studies.

MODERN GREEK STUDIES ASSOCIATION SERIES

1 *Modern Greek Writers,* Edmund Keeley and Peter Bien, Editors (Princeton University Press, Princeton, N.J., 1972)

2 *Hellenism and the First Greek War of Liberation, 1821–1830: Continuity and Change,* N. Diamandouros, J. Anton, J. Petropulos, and P. Toping, Editors (Institute for Balkan Studies, Thessaloniki, 1976)

3 *The "Past" in Medieval and Modern Greek Culture,* Speros Vryonis, Jr., Editor (UNDENA Publications, Malibu, Calif., 1978)

4 *Greece in the 1940s: A Nation in Crisis,* John O. Iatrides, Editor (University Press of New England, Hanover, N.H., 1981)

5 *Greece in the 1940s: A Bibliographic Companion,* John O. Iatrides, Editor (University Press of New England, Hanover, N.H., 1981)

Greece in the 1940s
A Bibliographic Companion

John O. Iatrides, Editor

Bibliographies by

Hagen Fleischer · Steven Bowman

University Press of New England

Hanover and London, 1981

UNIVERSITY PRESS OF NEW ENGLAND

BRANDEIS UNIVERSITY

BROWN UNIVERSITY

CLARK UNIVERSITY

DARTMOUTH COLLEGE

UNIVERSITY OF NEW HAMPSHIRE

UNIVERSITY OF RHODE ISLAND

TUFTS UNIVERSITY

UNIVERSITY OF VERMONT

Library of Congress Catalog Card Number 80-54473
International Standard Book Number 0-87451-199-2
Printed in the United States of America
Library of Congress Cataloging in Publication data
will be found on the last printed page of this book.

Contents

Classification System for Secondary Sources

/1/ Urban resistance (strike, sabotage, espionage, etc.)

/2/ Guerrilla warfare

/3/ Occupation and collaborationist authorities

/4/ Middle East (Government-in-exile, and its armed forces)

/5/ Memoirs and reminiscences

/6/ Based partially on reminiscences

/7/ Refers only in part to the occupation period

/8/ Key work

/R/ Right-wing source

/L/ Left-wing source

Preface

In the fall of 1978 the Modern Greek Studies Association (MGSA) devoted its biennial symposium to the turbulent decade of the 1940s and its impact upon Greece. Cosponsored by the Center for Mediterranean Studies of the American University, the event attracted considerable notice and was attended by several hundred scholars from North America and Europe. Many of the papers presented in the history and social sciences panels of the symposium have now been published in John O. Iatrides, editor, *Greece in the 1940s. A Nation in Crisis* (MGSA Series Volume 4, University Press of New England, 1981). Those involved in the preparation of that publication agreed that a separate companion volume, containing recently assembled bibliographical information on the same general subject, would be valuable to students of contemporary Greek history. *Greece in the 1940s. A Bibliographic Companion* is the result of that decision.

Hagen Fleischer initially prepared his bibliographical survey on "Greece under the Axis Occupation, 1941–1944," at the invitation of the editors of the *Modern Greek Society. A Social Science Newsletter,* an independent semi-annual publication sponsored by MGSA, where it appeared in two segments: Volume V, No. 1 (December 1977), and Volume VI, No. 1 (December 1978). For publication in the present volume Dr. Fleischer has updated and expanded the bibliography with the inclusion of more than two hundred additional entries. Steven Bowman's select annotated bibliography on the Jews of wartime Greece is the product of years of study and was part of an essay on the same subject which he presented at the 1978 MGSA symposium. Dr. Bowman has similarly edited and expanded his manuscript for inclusion in this publication.

Work on this volume has been guided by a number of considerations that may be briefly stated here.

The decision to publish these two important bibliographies was based entirely on their timely availability and does not reflect a deliberate choice in the particular topics to be covered. Indeed, it is unfortunate that a much more comprehensive bibliography of the 1940s, dealing as well with the Metaxas regime, the Greek-Italian war, the post-liberation period, the civil war and the American involvement in Greek affairs, has not been written. Perhaps this modest beginning will create the impetus for the much more ambitious project that is sorely needed.

As every scholar knows, judgments offered in the context of an annotated bibliography are as sound as their author is knowledgeable and objective. Furthermore, a degree of selectivity and arbitrariness is probably unavoidable in works of this kind. In publishing the two bibliographies the MGSA attests to their importance and usefulness as research tools, but assumes no responsibility for the views they contain.

The two bibliographers worked separately and followed somewhat different styles. This is especially noticeable in the matter of transliteration generally and the rendering of names in particular. Thus Hadzis in one may be Chadzis in the other and the equivalent (and derivatives) of John may appear alternatively as Yiannes, Yiannis, or Ioannis, and of George as Georgios, Georgos, or Giorgos. To avoid disturbing the bibliographer's alphabetical order no attempt has been made to adopt a uniform transliteration formula. Readers searching for particular entries should scan the two bibliographies in order to become familiar with the spelling and transliteration practices of the two authors.

Credit for making this volume possible belongs first of all to Hagen Fleischer and Steven Bowman. In addition, I wish to thank the editors of *Modern Greek Society*, Nikiforos Diamandouros, George Mavrogordatos, and Peter Allen, for permission to reproduce Dr. Fleischer's bibliography in its expanded version. Lily Macrakis, MGSA president during 1977–1979, and Peter Bien, chairman of the association's publications committee, were most helpful in many practical ways. Finally, I am grateful to Thomas L. McFarland, director of The University Press of New England, and Barbara Ras, managing editor, for their expert handling of the two-volume project and for turning what could have been tedious work into a pleasant undertaking.

November, 1980 John O. Iatrides
Cheshire, Connecticut

Part One

Greece under the Axis Occupation

A Bibliographical Survey

Hagen Fleischer

Introduction

More than thirty-five years after the end of the Second World War there still exists only one major bibliography covering to some extent the early literature on the occupation of Greece (Spencer, *infra*). But this very useful study deals only with a portion of the relevant books published before 1952; articles are entirely excluded. Other existing references are a concise essay published in 1948 (Stavrianos and Panagopoulos, *infra*) and a short catalog that focuses on the southeastern area of Europe (Hillgruber, *infra*). Beyond these works the scholar is left with brief listings in more recent publications or must rely on time-consuming search in libraries and elsewhere. Thus far there has been no official interest in Greece for an urgently needed, thorough compilation of sources, and private efforts in this direction have met with little encouragement.

In view of the prolonged neglect of such an important subject, the present survey provides the basis for a truly comprehensive bibliography. The first part of the survey covers unpublished primary sources; the second contains published primary sources; and the third includes memoirs and secondary works. Any attempt to distinguish between primary and secondary sources is always difficult and subject to question. Though I forgo any attempt to justify my choice in this matter, I will note by way of explanation that I have classified as primary sources all wartime materials because each such publication, whether produced legally or clandestinely, breathes in its special way the "spirit of the age." Each one of these sources provides us with a small but valuable fragment for the solution of that elusive, if not eternal, puzzle: the comprehension of an era.

Similarly, I have cited a considerable number of clandestine journals in order to provide clues for those willing to take the time and trouble to hunt down such rare but indispensable sources, most of which have not yet been closely examined by researchers. Obviously, such a list is far from complete. For example, there existed throughout occupied Greece a great variety of small, local presses, and different periodicals circulated among the employees of several government departments, among the workers in large industrial plants, and even among those confined to hospitals and sanatoria. Each of these publications concerned itself primarily with the special problems of its intended audience, and any attempt to offer a complete compilation of such materials is bound to fail.

I regret that I have been compelled to omit from these pages another group of valuable sources: the vast number of German, Italian, British, and especially Greek wartime leaflets. The classification of these various small publications would have required far too much space and would have introduced problems connected with diversity of issues and by the peculiarities of the publications themselves: many leaflets are undated and untitled, and many were written anonymously or pseudonymously, thus making their source a matter of speculation.

In listing unpublished materials my sole purpose is to provide scholars with an elementary guide to the sources. I have, therefore, confined myself to the major items and have not attempted to catalog fully all the files that I have consulted in the course of my research. Such a listing will be included in my work, "Greece 1941–1944, A Political History" (working title), a monograph soon to be published in German and Greek. In particular, full presentation of the files containing German wartime records would have proved especially lengthy, since it would have required the use of a triple classification system indicating: (1) the original (wartime) German file numbers; (2) the U.S. microfilm numbers; and (3) the new German classification symbols. (The new German classification system was rendered necessary by the separation and rearrangement of part of these files after their return to Germany.)

The National Archives in Washington, D.C., holds a nearly complete set of these German files in microfilm form. Information regarding the files can be obtained either from the *Guide to German Records* prepared by the archives staff, or from George O. Kent, ed., *A Catalogue of Files and Microfilms of the German Foreign Ministry Archives, 1920–1945*, volume III, (Stanford, California: Hoover Institution, 1966).

Other valuable collections are in the possession of various protagonists and minor figures of the occupation, or in the hands of their surviving relatives. A certain talent in gentle persuasion is necessary if one is intent on examining such collections.

Finally, I should like to note the existence of other pertinent unpublished materials besides those which I have personally examined and mentioned in this survey. Most important among these are the materials in the Italian Archives, those in the archives of the International Red Cross in Geneva, and the ones in the archives of those neutral states (Turkey, Spain, Argentina, and Switzerland) that maintained a diplomatic presence in occupied Greece and became involved in various relief and humanitarian activities, including attempts to rescue Jews. Unfortunately, the diplomatic records of former Axis satellites, such as Hungary and Bulgaria, are not at present accessible to the researcher.

Memoirs and other sources, which attempt an *a posteriori* reconstruction of events, almost inevitably require more extensive, and often more critical, annotations than the more contemporary documents listed in part one. Limitations of space, however, have often made it difficult to provide a thorough and objective evaluation of the works commented upon. As a result, it sometimes becomes necessary to mention errors, but not the fact that most of the writing is otherwise sound. Moreover, I hope to have avoided personal bias as much as possible.

Generally, the annotations refer solely to that part of a publication that relates to the subject of this bibliography, namely, the occupation period (1941–1944). When a work goes beyond that period (thematically or temporally), it is characterized by the symbol /7/. The classification system used herein represents an attempt to inform without taking up too much space, particularly in cases where the contents are not clearly defined by the title. Works characterized by the symbol /8/ (key works) are those I consider indispensable to the study of the occupation or some aspect thereof. The symbols /R/ (Right-wing source) and /L/ (Left-wing source) are dependent on interpretation, but they too are designed to provide basic information on the contents (especially of Greek writings), rather than merely to label political views.

Finally, some additional "technical" clarifications are necessary: (1) Some ex-guerrilla authors mention, along with their surname, their former pseudonym, which is provided herein in parentheses. Others write pseudonymously or even anonymously. In these cases, the real name—if known—is given in brackets. (2) The publisher is normally specified only if the work is still likely to be available. (3) Dates have been rendered according to the European system (day-month-year).

Acronyms and Abbreviations

AAA ’Αγών ’Απελευθερώσεως, ’Αναγεννήσεως [Struggle for Liberation, for Revival]

AE ’Αγωνιζομένη ‘Ελλάς [Fighting Greece]

AKE ’Αγροτικό Κόμμα ‘Ελλάδας [Agrarian Party of Greece]

AOK Armee-Oberkommando

ASKE ’Αγροτικό Σοσιαλδημοκρατικό Κόμμα τῆς ‘Ελλάδος [Agrarian Social Democratic Party of Greece]

ASO ’Αντιφασιστική Στρατιωτική ’Οργάνωση [Anti-Fascist Military Organization]

BLO British Liaison Officer

CC Central Committee

DKK Διεθνιστικό Κομμουνιστικό Κόμμα [International Communist Party]

EA ’Εθνική ’Αλληλεγγύη [National Solidarity]

EAM ’Εθνικό ’Απελευθερωτικό Μέτωπο [National Liberation Front]

ED ’Εθνική Δρᾶσις [National Action]

EDA Ἑνιαία Δημοκρατική ’Αριστερά [United Republican Left]

EDEM ’Εθνικόν Δημοκρατικόν ’Ελευθερωτικόν Μέτωπον [National Republican Liberation Front]

EDES ’Εθνικός Δημοκρατικός Ἑλληνικός Σύνδεσμος [National Republican Greek League]

EDFN ’Επαναστατική Δημοκρατική Φοιτητική Νεολαία [Revolutionary Republican Students’ Youth]

EDN ’Εθνική Δράση Νέων [National Youth Action]

EE ’Εθνικοκοινωνική ’Επανάστασις [National-Social Revolution]

EEAM ’Εθνικό ’Εργατικό ’Απελευθερωτικό Μέτωπο [Workers’ National Liberation Front]

EES ’Εθνικός Ἑλληνικός Στρατός [National Greek Army]

EK	Ἐθνικό Κομιτᾶτο [National Committee]
EKKA	Ἐθνική καί Κοινωνική Ἀπελευθέρωση [National and Social Liberation]
ELAS	Ἑλληνικός Λαϊκός Ἀπελευθερωτικός Στρατός [National Peoples' Liberation Army]
ELD	Ἕνωση Λαϊκῆς Δημοκρατίας [Union of Peoples' Democracy]
ENAM	Ἐθνικό Ναυτεργατικό Ἀπελευθερωτικό Μέτωπο [Naval Workers' National Liberation Front]
EOEA	Ἐθνικές Ὁμάδες Ἑλλήνων Ἀνταρτῶν [National Bands of Greek Guerrillas]
EOK	Ἐθνική Ὀργάνωσις Κρήτης [National Organization of Crete]
EPON	Ἑνιαία Πανελλαδική Ὀργάνωση Νέων [United Panhellenic Organization of Youth]
ESON	Ἐπαναστατική Σοσιαλιστική Ὀργάνωση Νέων [Revolutionary Socialist Youth Organization]
ESKKE	Ἐπαναστατικό Σοσιαλιστικό (Κομμουνιστικό) Κόμμα Ἑλλάδας [Revolutionary Socialist (Communist) Party of Greece]
ETA	Ἐπιμελητεία τοῦ Ἀντάρτη [Guerrilla's Commissariat]
EVEN	Ἕνωσις Βασιλοφρόνων Ἐθνικιστῶν Νέων [Union of Royalist Nationalist Youth]
GHQ	General Headquarters
HMSO	His (Her) Majesty's Stationery Office
HQ	Headquarters
IT	Ἱερή Ταξιαρχία [Sacred Brigade]
J.	Journal
KAKE	Κομμουνιστικό Ἀρχειομαρξιστικό Κόμμα Ἑλλάδος [Communist Party of Greece—Marxist Archive]
KE	Κόμμα Ἐργασίας [Labor Party]
KEA	Κόμμα Ἐθνικοκοινωνικῆς Ἀνασυγκροτήσεως [Party of National and Social Reconstruction]
KKE	Κομμουνιστικό Κόμμα Ἑλλάδας [Communist Party of Greece]

KOA Κομματική 'Οργάνωση 'Αθήνας [Party Organization of Athens]

LAE Λαϊκή 'Απελευθερωτική Ένωση [Peoples' Liberation Union]

LEO Λαϊκή 'Επαναστατική 'Οργάνωση [Peoples' Revolutionary Organization]

n.d. no date

n.p. no place

NP Νεοδημοκρατική Πρωτοπορεία [Neorepublican Vanguard]

OEE 'Οργάνωσις 'Ελευθέρων Ἑλλήνων [Organization of Free Greeks]

OKW Oberkommando der Wehrmacht

OSS Office of Strategic Services (U.S.)

OVA 'Οργάνωσις Βασιλοφρόνων 'Αγωνιστῶν [Organization of Royalist Fighters]

PA-ME Πατριωτικό Μέτωπο [Patriotic Front]

PAO Πανελλήνιος 'Απελευθερωτική 'Οργάνωσις [Panhellenic Liberation Organization]

PEAN Πανελλήνιος Ένωσις 'Αγωνιζομένων Νέων [Panhellenic Union of Fighting Youth]

PEEA Πολιτική 'Επιτροπή 'Εθνικῆς 'Απελευθέρωσης [Political Committee of National Liberation]

POES Πατριωτική 'Οργάνωση 'Ελεύθεροι Σκλάβοι [Patriotic Organization Free Slaves]

RAN Ρωμυλία—Αὐλών—Νῆσοι [Rumelia—Avlona—Isles] An acronym indicating the organization's territorial claims for Greater Greece

RO Ριζοσπαστική 'Οργάνωση [Radical Organization]

SEO Σύνδεσμος 'Εθνικῶν 'Οργανώσεων [League of Nationalist Organizations]

SOE Special Operations Executive (British)

SSN Στρατιά Σκλαβομένων Νικητῶν [Army of Enslaved Victors]

VNE Βασιλική Νεολαία Ἑλλάδος [Royalist Youth of Greece]

I. Unpublished Primary Sources

A. GERMAN RECORDS

1. Wartime Materials

a. Auswärtiges Amt, Politisches Archiv (Bonn)

The extant papers of the following departments contain documents on occupied Greece:

Büro Reichsminister
Büro Staatssekretär
Büro Unterstaatssekretär
Handelspolitische Abteilung
Politische Abteilung
Abteilung Inland
Protokollar-Abteilung
Sonderkommando v. Künsberg

Only a very small portion of documents has been published in the two selective editions cited in section II, C, (*Akten . . . , Documents . . .)*. Thus, search in the unpublished files or microfilms (see, E1 *infra*) becomes essential for an understanding of the political situation in occupied Greece.

b. Bundesarchiv (Koblenz)

Contains most German records with the exception of political (1a, supra), army (1c), and personal files (1e). See:

Reichsfinanzministerium
Reichswirtschaftsministerium
Reichskanzlei
Reichssicherheitshauptamt
Persönlicher Stab Reichsführer SS
Chef der Ordnungspolizei
Deutsche Polizeidienststellen in den besetzten und eingegliederten Gebieten
Südosteuropa-Gesellschaft
Deutsch-Griechische Warenausgleichsgesellschaft
Bevollmächtigter der Reiches für Griechenland
Sonderbevollmächtigter des Reiches für den Südosten, Dienststelle Athen

c. Bundesarchiv—Militärarchiv (Freiburg)

Regarding the German military authorities and units serving in occupied Greece, see, for more details, Heinz Richter, *Modern Greek Society: A Newsletter,* 4 (May 1975), 45–50. If possible, the authoritative *Guides to German Records Microfilmed at Alexandria, Va.* (Washington, D.C., 1958 ff.) should be consulted. Unfortunately, during the last phase of the war, many records were, whether willingly or not, destroyed, and thus the pertinent papers of some units no longer exist. Nevertheless, the extant records—at least those originating from the German intelligence staff (Ic)—are essential to any scholarly study of Greek resistance.

With reference to occupied Greece, files from the following military authorities have been preserved:

i. Wehrmacht, High Command
OKW, Wehrmachtsführungsstab
OKW, Wehrwirtschafts—und Rüstungsamt

ii. Armies and Army Groups (Tactical Commanders)*

*Responsibility for tactical and territorial command was not clearly separated, causing a nearly continuous inner-German conflict of jurisdiction.

AOK 12 (= Wehrmachtbefehlshaber Südost), replaced as of 1 January 1943 by:
Heeresgruppe E (= Oberbefehlshaber Südost) whose responsibility was, after 25 August 1943, limited to Greece (and Northern Epirus), while the Balkan High Command was assumed by the newly established:
Heeresgruppe F (= Oberbefehlshaber Südost).

iii. Territorial Commanders and comparable authorities
Befehlshaber Südgriechenland after 25 August 1943 renamed:
Militärbefehlshaber Griechenland
Befehlshaber Saloniki-Ägäis
Kommandant Festung Kreta
Kommandant Ost-Ägäis (see v. *infra*)

After 13 August 1943, all the aforementioned territorial command authorities, with the exception of a vague semi-autonomous status for Crete and "Ost-Ägäis" (Dodecanese, Samos, Icaria, etc.), were subordinated to:
Militärbefehlshaber Südost
Admiral Ägäis
Wehrmachtsbefehlshaber Mazedonien

iv. Army Corps and comparable authorities
XVIII. Armee korps
Deutscher Generalstab beim italienischen AOK 11
Renamed, on 9 September 1943, as:
Armeegruppe Südgriechenland
Merged on 5 October 1943 with
LXVIII. Armeekorps.
XXII. Armeekorps
LXXXXI. Armeekorps (zur besonderen Verwendung)

v. Divisions
1. Panzer-Division
1. Gebirgs-Division
11. Luftwaffen-Felddivision
22. Infanterie-Division
117. Jäger-Division
Festungsdivision Kreta
Sturmdivision Rhodos (= Kommandant Ost-Ägäis, *supra*)
In addition, scattered records of several subunits (regiments, battalions) and minor authorities ("Kreis-Kommandantur" etc.) are also included in this archive.

d. Institut für Zeitgeschichte (Munich)
Miscellaneous records and other pertinent material.

e. Berlin Document Center (West Berlin)
Personal files of National Socialist Party (and affiliated organizations) members. (Still restricted; only files of "historical interest" may be seen after having obtained permission by the "Senator für Inneres" [D-1000 Berlin 31]).

2. Post-war records of judicial proceedings and Related Collections These records contain, in part, original war documents.

a. Records of the U.S. Nuremberg War Crime Trials.
In particular, see case 7, "Hostage Case" (United States of America v. Wilhelm List, et al.—i.e., the generals who had served in South East Europe).
The following agencies, among others, possess more or less complete sets of these huge files:
Staatliches Archivlager (Göttingen)
Staatsarchiv Nürnberg
Institut für Zeitgeschichte (Munich), see also: 1d, supra
Geheimes Staatsarchiv Dahlem (West Berlin)
Max Planck Institut für Völkerrecht (Heidelberg)
U.S. National Archives, Washington, D.C.

b. Records of German Preliminary Proceedings Relating to War Crimes in Occupied Greece.

The files of the numerous cases, containing informative testimonies, documents, etc., are dispersed, depending on local jurisdiction, in the depositories of many German prosecuting courts (Staatsanwaltschaft). Information as to the location of individual files can be obtained from the Zentrale Stelle der Landesjustizverwaltungen zur Aufklärung nationalsozialistischer Verbrechen (Ludwigsburg).

Access to the files of closed cases requires the prior consent of the responsible Provincial Ministry of Justice (Landesjustizministerium). Varying degrees of patience and perseverance are needed before such consent is obtained.

c. Dokumentationsarchiv des Österreichischen Widerstandes (Vienna)

Affidavits and interviews by Austrian soldiers who served in occupied Greece and who, in part, cooperated with EAM/ELAS.

B. BRITISH RECORDS

1. Public Record Office (London)

War Cabinet Papers
(Series CAB 65, CAB 66, passim)

Foreign Office Papers
(Series F.O. 371)

War Office Papers
(largely closed)

2. University of London, King's College. Liddell Hart Centre for Military Archives

C.M. Woodhouse, Personal Papers

E.C.W. Myers, Personal Papers

British records, and especially F.O. papers, are indispensable for any student of Greek history during the Second World War.

C. SWEDISH RECORDS

Utrikesdepartementet [Foreign Ministry] (Stockholm):

Swedish Embassy, Athens

Swedish Embassy, Sofia

Swedish Foreign Ministry

D. ITALIAN RECORDS

U.S. National Archives

For information on the scattered files on Greece contained in the Archives in microfilm form, see, *Guide to Records of the Italian Armed Forces.* 3 vols. (Washington, D.C.: National Archives, 1967).

E. UNITED STATES RECORDS

1. U.S. National Archives (Washington, D.C.)

Department of State

Office of Strategic Services

War Department General and Special Staffs

Military Intelligence Division

Naval Intelligence Division

In addition:

Microfilms of most German record funds cited in:

IA1. a–c, 2a. (*supra*)

See also: Italian Records (ID, *supra*).

Franklin D. Roosevelt Library (Hyde Park, New York)

Franklin D. Roosevelt Papers

Harry L. Hopkins Papers

F. GREEK RECORDS

The Greek Foreign Ministry records are still closed because of the fifty-year rule. As a result, diplomatic papers can only be consulted in collections originating from private holdings. The most essential of these consists of the Emmanuel Tsouderos files and is divided up between the Gennadios Library (Athens) and the General State Archives. Supplementary, and in part duplicate, material can be found at St. Antony's College (Oxford), in the private papers of Ch. Simopoulos, Greek Ambassador to Britain and Foreign Under-Secretary in the Tsouderos government. They cover the period until Simopoulos' death, in October 1942.

Several private collections are kept at the Benaki Museum (Athens), e.g., the papers of A. Benakes and N. Deas. Voluminous material on many resistance organizations is contained in the Military Archives of the Greek General Staff. For the most, however, it consists of self-praising post-war accounts written by representatives of the entire spectrum of nationalist organizations. The "nationalist resistance" activities of the German-founded Security Battalions figure prominently in these files.

Finally, it should be noted that many municipal archives have preserved some files on the activities of Italian or German occupation authorities.

II. Published Primary Sources

A. OFFICIAL BULLETINS

Allgemeine Heeresmitteilungen (edited by Oberkommando des Heeres).

Δελτίον Πληροφοριῶν [Information Bulletin] (edited by the Greek Office of Information, Washington, D.C.), typewritten-mimeographed.

Department of State, Bulletin

Deutsche Nachrichten in Griechenland (semi-official)

'Εφημερίς τῆς Κυβερνήσεως τοῦ Βασιλείου τῆς 'Ελλάδος [Government Gazette of the Kingdom of Greece] (Johannesburg, London, Cairo).

'Ελληνική Πολιτεία, 'Εφημερίς τῆς Κυβερνήσεως [Greek Republic, Government Gazette] (Athens) Publication of the collaborationist government.

Gazetta Ionica and *'Εφημερίς τῶν 'Ιωνίων*, (edited by the Italian Office of Political Affairs in the Ionian Islands). Circulated both in Greek and in Italian.

Verordnungsblatt des Befehlshabers Saloniki-Ägäis

Verordnungsblatt für das Besetzte Griechische Gebiet (edited by the Oberbefehlshaber Südost).

Verordnungsblatt für Griechenland (edited by the Militärbefehlshaber Griechenland). The last three bulletins are bilingual (Greek-German)

B. SOURCES OF GREEK PROVENANCE

1. Clandestine Publications

a. Newspapers and Periodicals

The organization responsible for the publication of each item listed is identified immediately following the bracketed translation of the respective title.

'Αγροτική Φωνή [Agrarian Voice]. ASKE CC.

'Αγροτικό Βῆμα [Agrarian Tribune]. AKE

'Αγωνιζομένη 'Ελλάς [Fighting Greece]. AE

'Αγωνιστής [The Fighter]. EAM, Yannina

'Αλληλεγγύη [Solidarity]. EA, Roumeli

'Αντιφασίστας [Anti-Fascist]. ASO, Cairo

'Απελευθέρωση [Liberation]. EKKA CC

'Αστυνομικό Βῆμα [Police Tribune]. EAM, police branch

Γυναικεία Δράση [Women's Action]. EAM

Δελτίο Πράξεων καί 'Αποφάσεων [Bulletin of Acts and Decisions]. PEEA

Δεσμώτης 'Ελλην [Captive Greek]. KEA

Δημοκρατία [Republic]. np

Δημοκρατική Σημαία [Republican Flag]. EDES, Athens

Δημοκρατική Φλόγα [Republican Flame]. EDFN

Διαρκής 'Επανάσταση [Permanent Revolution]. DKK

Δόξα [Glory]. PEAN

Ε.Δ.Ε.Μ. [E.D.E.M.]. EDEM

Ε.Δ.Ε.Σ. [E.D.E.S.]. EDES

Ε.Ε. [E.E.]. EE

'Εθνική 'Αλληλεγγύη [National Solidarity]. EA, CC

'Εθνική Πνοή [National Breath]. EDES, Preveza

'Εθνική Φλόγα [National Flame]. EDES, GHQ, Epirus

'Εθνική Φωνή [National Voice]. PAO, Thessaloniki
'Εθνικός 'Αγών [National Struggle]. AAA
'Εθνικός 'Αγωνιστής [National Fighter]. OVA
'Εθνικός Δρόμος [National Way]. EVEN
'Ελεύθερα 'Επτάνησα [Free Ionian Islands]. EAM, Ionian Islands
'Ελευθέρα 'Ορεινή 'Ελλάς [Free Mountain Greece]. GHQ EDES, Epirus
'Ελεύθερη 'Ελλάδα [Free Greece]. EAM CC
'Ελεύθερη 'Ελληνική Ψυχή [Free Greek Soul]. Spitha (metaxist)
'Ελεύθερη Ζωή [Free Life]. KE
'Ελεύθερη Ρούμελη [Fre Rumeli]. EAM, Lamia
'Ελεύθερη Σκέψη [Free Thought]. EK
'Ελευθερία [Freedom]. KKE, Yannina
'Ελεύθεροι—Σκλάβοι [Free—Slaves]. POES
'Ελευθερωτής [Liberator]. ELAS, HQ Peloponnesus
'Ελληνικά Νειάτα [Greek Youth]. IT
'Ελληνικόν Αἷμα [Greek Blood]. Hellenikon Aima
'Ελληνικός 'Αγών [Greek Struggle]. EDES, Epirus
'Εμπρός [Forward]. EAM, Athens
'Εμπρός [Forward]. EPON, Lamia
'Εμπρός [Forward]. KKE, Athens: Private Clerks' Branch
'Εμπρός [Forward]. SEO
'Επαναστάτης [Revolutionary]. PEAN
'Επιμελητεία [Comissariat]. ETA, CC
'Εργατικό Βῆμα [Workers' Tribune]. EEAM, CC
'Εργατικός 'Αγώνας [Workers' Struggle]. EEAM, Athens Committee
Ε.Σ.Ο.Ν. [E.S.O.N.]. ESON
'Εσωκομματικό Δελτίο [Internal Party Bulletin]. KKE, KOA
'Εφημερίς τῆς 'Ελλάδος [Gazette of Greece]. No indication regarding publisher; apparently liberal.
'Η 'Αλήθεια [The Truth]. [United Party]
'Η 'Επανάσταση [The Revolution]. EDES, Epirus
'Η 'Εφοδος [The Assault]. ED
'Η Μάχη [The Battle]. ED
'Η Μάχη [The Battle]. ELD
'Η Μαχομένη 'Ελλάς [Fighting Greece]. Sometimes also *Μαχομένη 'Ελλάς*. No indication regarding publisher. Sympathetic to PEAN.
'Η Μπόμπα [The Bomb.] Promachoi
'Η Ρουμελιώτισα [The Woman of Roumeli]. EAM, Central Greece
'Η Φωνή τοῦ EAM [The Voice of EAM]. EAM, Karditsa
Καραμανιόλος [Karamaniolos]. EAM, Samos
Κόκκινη Σημαία [Red Flag]. ESKKE, CC
Κόκκινη Σημαία [Red Flag]. KKE, Thessalian Bureau
Κομμουνιστική 'Επιθεώρηση [Communist Review]. KKE, CC
Λ.Α.Ε. [L.A.E.]. LAE
Λαϊκή Φωνή [People's Voice]. KKE, Macedonian Bureau (Thessaloniki)
Λευτεριά [Freedom]. EAM, Euboea
Λευτεριά [Freedom]. KKE, KOA
Λεύτερος Μωρηάς [Free Peloponnesus]. KKE, Peloponnesus
Μαχητής [Fighter]. EPON, Karpenisi
Μεγάλη 'Ελλάς [Greater Greece]. SSN
Μηνιάτικος 'Αντάρτης [Monthly Guerrilla]. ELAS 13th Division
Νέα Γενιά [New Generation]. EPON
Νέα 'Ελλάδα [New Greece]. EAM, Athens
'Ο 'Αγώνας μας [Our Struggle]. DKK, CC
'Ο 'Αγωνιστής [The Fighter]. EDN
'Ο 'Αντάρτης [The Guerrilla]. ELAS, HQ Central Greece
'Ο 'Απελευθερωτής [The Liberator]. ELAS, CC

'Οδηγητής [Guide]. KKE, Bureau of Central Greece

O.E.E. [O.E.E.]. OEE

'Ο 'Εκδικητής [The Avenger]. ELAS, Attica-Boeotia

'Ο Λενινιστής [The Leninist]. KKE, Thessalian Bureau (for internal use)

'Ο Μαχητής [The Fighter]. KKE, KOA

'Ο Πατριωτης [The Patriot]. PA-ME

'Ο Προμαχων [The Rampart]. Promachoi

'Οργανωτής [The Organizer]. KKE, CC (for internal use)

'Ο Συνεχιστής [The Continuer]. Synechistai, moderately socialist

Πάλη [Struggle]. KKE, Lamia

Πάλη τῶν τάξεων [Class Struggle]. KAKE, CC

Παρόν [Present]. No indication regarding publisher. Liberal

Πρωτοπόροι [Vanguard]. EAM, Athens

Ριζοσπάστης [Radical]. KKE, CC. As of spring 1944, two editions: in Athens and in the "mountains"

P.O. [R.O.]. RO

Ρούμελη [Roumeli]. EAM, Central Greece

Σημαία [Flag]. VNE

Σοβιετικά Νέα [Soviet News]. KKE, KOA

Στέμμα [Crown]. EE (No. 1 being the continuation of E.E. No. 19)

4 Αὐγούστου, 'Η Φωνή τῆς Πατρίδος [4th August, the Voice of the Fatherland]. EE

Τό Δελτίο [The Bulletin]. No indication regarding publisher. [Dem. Tsimbos]

Φλόγα [Flame]. EPON, Students' Branch

Φλόγα [Flame]. KKE, Lokrida

Φλόγα (sometimes *'Η φλόγα*) [(The) Flame]. np

Φρουροί Βορείου 'Ελλάδος [Sentinels of Northern Greece]. AE

Φωνή τοῦ Λαοῦ [People's Voice]. KKE, Euboea

Φωνή τοῦ Λαοῦ [People's Voice]. LEO

Φωνή τῶν Νέων [Voice of the Young]. EPON, Yannina

Φωνή τοῦ Φεραίου [Pheraios' Voice]. EPON, Central Greece

b. Pamphlets and other non-periodical issues

R = has been reprinted, mostly after 1974.

RR = has been repeatedly reprinted; the first reprint appeared during the occupation.

These indications are intended only as auxiliary means of identification and are not necessarily complete.

Demokratike Omada. *Οἱ ἐθνικές μας διεκδικήσεις* [Our National Claims] (Athens, 1 October 1944).

EAM CC. [=Glenos, Demetres]. *Τί εἶναι καί τί θέλει τό 'Εθνικό 'Απελευθερωτικό Μέτωπο* [What Is the National Liberation Movement and What Are Its Aims] (Athens, Sept. 1942). RR

EAM CC. *Πῶς πρέπει νά δουλεύει ἡ γυναίκα στό 'Εθνικό 'Απελευθερωτικό Μέτωπο* [How Women Should Work in the National Liberation Front]. (n.p., Febr. 1943). R

EAM CC. *Τί εἶναι ὁ Λαϊκός Στρατός* [What is the People's Army]. (n.p., n.d.=1943).

EAM CC. *Τίποτε κρυφό ἀπό τόν 'Ελληνικό Λαό* [Nothing Is Hidden from the Greek People] (Athens, November 1943).

EAM CC. *Τά 'Αετόπουλα. 'Αναγνωστικό γ' καί δ' τάξης* [The Eaglets. Reading Book for 3rd and 4th Grades] (n.p., 1944). RR

EAM CC. *Τό EAM συνεπής ὑπερασπιστής τῆς ἐθνικῆς ἑνότητας. Οἱ διαπραγματεύσεις τοῦ EAM-ΕΛΑΣ μέ τόν ΕΔΕΣ καί τήν ΕΚΚΑ* [EAM: The Responsible Defender of

National Unity. The Negotiations of EAM-ELAS with EDES and EKKA] (n.p., March 1944).

EAM/EPON. *Σχέδιο μιᾶς λαϊκῆς παιδείας. Εἰσήγηση τοῦ ΕΑΜ καί τῆς ΕΠΟΝ στή γραμματεία παιδείας τῆς ΠΕΕΑ* [Project for a Popular Education. Proposals by EAM and EPON to the PEEA Education Secretariat] (n.p., 1944). R

EDES [= Pyromaglou, Komnenos]. *Τί εἶπα στόν Λίβανο* [What I said in the Lebanon] ("Free Mountain Greece", 1944).

———. *'Απάντηση εἰς τό ΕΑΜ-ΕΛΑΣ* [Reply to EAM-ELAS] ("Free Mountain Greece", 1944).
Literally the same text as in the previous brochure.

EKKA. *'Επίσημη Ἔκθεση τῆς ὀργάνωσης ΕΚΚΑ γιά τίς ἐπιθέσεις τοῦ ΕΑΜ-ΕΛΑΣ κατά τοῦ 5/42 Εὐζώνων καί τή δολοφονία τοῦ Συνταγματάρχη Ψαρροῦ* [The Official Report of the EKKA Organization concerning the Attacks of EAM-ELAS against the 5/42 Evzones and the Murder of Colonel Psarros] (Athens, June 1944).

ELAS CC [Makrides, Th.]. *'Ο 'Αντάρτης τοῦ ΕΑΜ-ΕΛΑΣ* [The Guerrilla of EAM-ELAS] (Athens, spring 1943).

ELAS, HQ Thessaly. *Γιά τή Λευτεριά, τήν Λαοκρατία* [For Freedom and People's Rule] (n.p., 1943).

ELAS, General Headquarters. *Ἕνας χρόνος τῆς Σχολῆς 'Εφ. 'Αξ/κῶν ΕΛΑΣ* [One Year since the Foundation of the ELAS Reserve Officers School] ("Free Greece," Aug. 1944). R

EK. *Τό 'Εθνικό Κομιτᾶτο . . . Τί εἶναι, τί πιστεύει, γιά τί ἀγωνίζεται* [The National Committee . . . , Its Nature, Its Creed, Its Aims] (Athens, 1941[?]).

ENAM. *'Εθνικό Προσκλητήριο πρός τούς Ἕλληνες Ναυτεργάτες* [The Nation's Call to the Greek Dock Workers] (Athens, July 1943).

Hellenikon Aima. *Τό ΕΑΜ ἀπέναντι τοῦ Ἔθνους* [The EAM Against the Nation] (Athens, July 1943). RR

———. A series of 30 brochures, published at irregular intervals (Athens, 1943–1944). 14 of them are reprinted in Peniatoglou, Vovolines (see B2 *infra*).

KKE CC. *Λαοκρατία καί Σοσιαλισμός* [People's Rule and Socialism] (Athens, spring 1943). RR

KKE CC. *Καταστατικό τοῦ ΚΚΕ* [Statutes of the KKE] (Athens, 1943). With comments.

KKE CC [= Y. Ioannides]. *'Η διάλυση τῆς Κομ. Διεθνοῦς καί ἡ πάλη γιά τή λεύτερη καί λαοκρατούμενη Ἑλλάδα* [The Dissolution of the Comintern and the Struggle for a Free Greece Ruled by the People] (Athens, June 1943).

KKE CC. *Τό 'Εθνικό μας πρόβλημα καί τό Κομμουνιστικό Κόμμα τῆς 'Ελλάδας* [Our National Problem and the Communist Party of Greece] (Athens, 1943). R

KKE CC. *6 'Απρίλη 1941–6 'Απρίλη 1944. Τρία χρόνια* "Νέας Τάξης" *καί τά χιτλερικά σώματα Τσολιάδων—Χωροφυλάκων—Χαφιέδων—ΕΕΕ κ.λ.π.* [6 April 1941–6 April 1944: Three Years of the "New Order" and the Hitlerite Forces of Evzones, Gendarmes, Narks, EEE, etc.] (Athens, 1944).

KKE CC. *Προδότες καί ἐγκληματίες* [Traitors and Criminals] (Athens, 1944). RR

KKE-KOA. *Ἔξι ἁπλά μαθήματα* [Six Simple Lessons] 3 brochures. (Athens, 1944).

KKE-KOA. *Ὅλα γιά τήν Ἐθνική Ἑνότητα. Ἡ 5η Συνδιάσκεψη τῆς Κομματικῆς Ὀργάνωσης τῆς Ἀθήνας τοῦ ΚΚΕ* [Everything for National Unity. The 5th Congress of the KKE Party Organization of Athens].

KKE, Macedonian Bureau. *Ἡ σκευωρία τοῦ Λιβάνου. Γλύξμπουργκ-Παπανδρέου ἀντιμέτωποι τοῦ ἔθνους* [The Lebanon Intrigue. Glücksburg—Papandreou Antagonists of the Nation] (Thessaloniki, July 1944). R

KKE, Thessalian Bureau, [= K. Karagiorges]. "Τρία χρόνια ἀγῶνες τοῦ Κομμουνιστικοῦ Κόμματος στή Θεσσαλία" [Three Years' Struggle of the Communist Party in Thessaly], *Ho Leninistes,* II: 9–10 (May–June 1944), 1–28.

[Lambrinos, G. and Avgeres, M.]. *Προβλήματα τῆς σημερινῆς τέχνης* [Problems of Today's Art] A proclamation edited by the "Literary Branch" of EAM, reprinted in *Aiolika Grammata,* V. 29, (1975) 358–362.

NP. *Γιά τήν ἄμυνα καί τήν ἀναγέννηση τοῦ Ἑλληνισμοῦ* [For the Defense and the Rebirth of Hellenism] (Athens, 1943).

[PAO]. *Ἕλληνες Πατριῶται* [Greek Patriots] (n.p.[= Thessaloniki], 1943).

PEAN. *Τί προσέφερε καί τί δικαιοῦται νά ζητήσει ἡ Ἑλλάς* [What Greece contributed and What She Is Entitled to Claim](n.p., n.d. [= Athens, 1943]).

Pesmazoglou, Michael, A. *Ἡ νομική φύσις τῆς ὑπό ἐχθρικήν στρατιωτικήν κατοχήν συγκροτηθείσης Ἑλληνικῆς κυβερνήσεως* [The Legal Nature of the Greek Government Constituted under Enemy Military Occupation] (Athens, 1942).

RAN. *Τό Ἑλληνικό πρόβλημα. Α. Τί ζητοῦμεν. Β Ὁ Βουλγαρικός φάκελος* [The Greek Problem. A. What We Demand. B. The Bulgarian File] (Athens, 1943).

Roussos, Petros. *Τό ΕΑΜ ἐλευθερωτής καί ἀναγεννητής τῆς Ἑλλάδας. Λόγος στήν πανηγυρική συγκέντρωση γιά τά τρίχρονα τοῦ ΕΑΜ στήν ἕδρα τῆς Κεντρικῆς Ἐπιτροπῆς, Ἐλεύθερη Ἑλλάδα, Ὀκτώβρης,* 1944. [The EAM, Liberator and Regenerator of Greece. Speech Delivered at the Panegyric Gathering on the Occasion of EAM's Third Anniversary at the Headquarters of the Central Committee. Free Greece, October 1944] (Phourna, 1944). R

Siantos, G. "Ἡ πορεία ἐξέλιξης τῆς ἐσωτερικῆς καί ἐξωτερικῆς κατάστασης ἀπ' τό 6ο Συνέδριο τοῦ Κομμουνιστικοῦ Κόμματος τῆς Ἑλλάδας (Δεκέμβρης 1935) *ὡς τήν Πανελλαδική Συνδιάσκεψη τοῦ ΚΚΕ (Δεκέμβρης* 1942), *ἡ δράση τοῦ ΚΚΕ μέσα σ'αὐτό τό χρονικό διάστημα καί τά ἀπό δῶ καί πέρα μεγάλα καθήκοντα τῶν Ἑλλήνων Κομμουνιστῶν*" [The Course of Developments of the Internal and External Situation from the 6th Congress of the Greek Communist Party (Dec. 1935) to the KKE Panhellenic Conference (Dec. 1942). The KKE Activities during this Period and the Future Great Duties of the Greek Communists], *Kommounistike Epitheorese,* 10 (February 1943), 1–30.

———. Many other articles (mostly anonymous) in *Kom. Ep.*

Velouchiotes, Ares [=Klaras, Thanases]. *Ὁ λόγος τῆς Λαμίας Ὀκτώβριος, 1944* [The Lamia Speech, October, 1944] (Athens: Hellenika Themata, 1974)

Zevgos, Yiannes. "Ἡ πορεία τοῦ πολέμου καί ἡ ἐξέλιξη τῆς πολιτικῆς κατάστασης ἀπό τήν Πανελλαδική Συνδιάσκεψη (Δεκέμβρης 1942) *καί ὁ δρόμος τοῦ ἀπελευθερωτικοῦ ἀγῶνα πρός τή νίκη*" [The Course of the War and the Development of the Political Situation from the Panhellenic Conference (Dec. 1942) and the Advance of the Liberation Struggle towards Victory], *Kommounistike Epitheorese*, 23 (February 1944), 1–39.

———. Many other articles (mostly anonymous).

2. Official Reports, Diaries, Collections of Documents and Other Pertinent Materials

Anagnostopoulos, Nik. A. *Παράνομος Τύπος* [Clandestine Press] (Athens, 1960).

Christides, Chr. *Χρόνια Κατοχῆς: 1941–1944. Μαρτυρίες Ἡμερολογίου* [Occupation Years, 1941–1944. A Diary's Testimony] (Athens: By the author, 1971).

———. ed. *Παῦλος Μών. Inter Arma Caritas. Ἀναμνήσεις ἀπό τήν Ἑλλάδα κατά τήν Κατοχή (1941–1944)* [Paul Mohn. Inter Arma Caritas. Memoirs from Greece During the Occupation (1941–1944)] (Nicosia: By the author, 1969).

Demetriades, Phokion. *Σκιά πάνω ἀπ'τήν Ἀθῆνα* 2nd ed.: (Athens, 1970); English edition: *Shadow Over Athens.* (New York and Toronto, 1946). Cartoons from the occupation years.

Dragoumes, Ph. *Ἐκλογή πολιτικῶν δημοσιευμάτων* [Selection of Political Publications] (Athens, 1945).

EAM. "Ἔκθεση τῆς ἐπιτροπῆς περιοχῆς Μακεδονίας τοῦ ΕΑΜ γιά τήν τρίχρονη ἐθνικοαπελευθερωτική πάλη τοῦ λαοῦ τῆς Μακεδονίας (10.8.1944)" [Report of the EAM Macedonian Regional Committee on the Three Year National Liberation Struggle of the Macedonian People (10 August 1944)], *Ethnike Antistase*, 4 (April 1963), 329–343.

EAM. "Ἐπίσημα Κείμενα σχετικά μέ τήν ὀργάνωση καί δράση Γερμανῶν Ἀντιφασιστῶν στρατιωτικῶν στήν κατεχομένη Ἑλλάδα" [Official Texts Concerning the Organization and Activity of German Anti-Fascist Soldiers in Occupied Greece], *Ethnike Antistase*, 9 (Dec. 1966), 917–930.

EAM. *Λευκή Βίβλος (Μάης 1944–Γενάρης 1945).* (Trikkala, Febr. 1945). Enlarged Reprint: *Λευκή Βίβλος. (Μάης 1944–Μάρτης 1945)* (Athens, 1945). English Edition: *White Book (May 1944–March 1945) (New York, 1945).*

EKKA, HQ Roumeli. "Ἐπίσημη ἔκθεσις"[Official Report], *Historike Epitheoresis*, 8–9 (1965), 296–301.

Ἐκτελεσθέντες ἐπί κατοχῆς. Ἀπό τά ἀρχεῖα τῆς Ἀρχιεπισκοπῆς [Those Who Were Executed during the Occupation. From the Archives of the Archdiocese] With a preface by Ioanna Tsatsou, (Athens, 1947).

ELAS, Group of Divisons in Macedonia. "Ἀπό τή δράση τῶν Ἄγγλων Συνδέσμων Ἀξιωματικῶν στόν ΕΛΑΣ Δυτικῆς Μακεδονίας" [From the Activities of the English Liaison Officers attached to the ELAS of West Macedonia], *Ethnike Antistase*, 2 (August 1962), 106–113.

ELAS, 10th Division. *3 ἐκθέσεις, 1944* [3 Roports 1944] *Ethnike Antistase*, 16 (August 1978), 5–11.

[Eliou, Philippos ed.] *Ὁ Ἄρης Βελουχιώτης & ἡ ἡγεσία τοῦ ΚΚΕ τό καλοκαίρι τοῦ 1943* [Ares Velouchiotes and the KKE Leadership in the Summer of 1943]. *Avge* 9.–12.9.79

Ares' views are expressed in two interesting reports to the politburo, the one written by himself (22.9.43), the other by Orpheas Vlachopoulos [P. Karagitses].

Eranistes, ed. "'Ασκήσεις μάχης τοῦ ἐφεδρικοῦ ΕΛΑΣ 'Αθήνας" [Manoeuvers of the ELAS Reserve in Athens], *Anti* 2.11.78, 22–34. A series of rare documents and some comments.

Evangelos, Metropolitan of Hermoupolis. *Θρησκευτικά καί πατριωτικά σαλπίσματα* [Religious and Patriotic Trumpet Calls] (Alexandria, 1947). The collection contains also memorial speeches given in the Middle East on the anniversaries of Metaxas' death.

Glenos, Demetrios. *Τά σημερινά προβλήματα τοῦ 'Ελληνισμοῦ* [The Problems Facing Hellenism Today]. With a preface by G. C. Zioutos. (Athens, 1945). Glenos' last notes before his sudden death in December 1943.

Gounarakes, Petros N. *Σελίδες τινές ἐπί τῆς ἐπεμβάσεως τῶν κυβερνήσεων κατοχῆς εἰς τά τῆς 'Εθνικῆς Τραπέζης τῆς 'Ελλάδος* [Some Pages concerning the Intervention of the Occupation Governments into the Affairs of the National Bank of Greece] (Athens, 1945).

Greece. Ministry of Social Welfare. *Καταστραφεῖσαι πόλεις καί χωρία συνεπεία τοῦ πολέμου 1940–1945* [Towns and Villages Destroyed as a Result of the War 1940–1945] (Athens, 1946).

Greece. Office National Hellénique des Criminels de Guerre. *Les atrocités des quatre envahisseurs de la Grèce.* (Athens, 1946).

Greece. Under-Secretariat for Press and Information. *The Conspiracy against Greece* (Athens, 1947). Greek edition: *'Η ἐναντίον τῆς 'Ελλάδος ἐπιβουλή* (Athens, 1947). Contains, among others, alleged proof of EAM/KKE "collaboration with the enemy" during the occupation years. Based mainly on fakes and on highly suspect "documents" "discovered" by Rightist organizations in 1943–1944.

Hadjipateras, Costas N. *Heroismes et droits de la Grèce* (Paris, 1946). Press articles and speeches of the period 1942–1946.

Ἥρωες καί Μάρτυρες [Heroes and Martyrs] (Athens: Nea Hellada, 1954). Short biographical summaries of about three thousand members of EAM, KKE, etc., who were executed or died in prison.

Kanellopoulos, Panagiotes. *'Ημερολόγιο. 31 Μαρτίου 1942–4 'Ιανουαρίου 1945* [Diary 31 March 1942–4 January 1945] (Athens: Kedros, 1977). Essential source for the events in the Middle East and for the "interregnum" in the Peloponnesus immediately after the German retreat.

Kirjazovski, R., Pejov, V. and Simovski, T. *Egejska Makedonija vo NOB 1944–1945* [Aegean Macedonia in the National Liberation Struggle 1944–1945] (Skopje: Arhiv na Makedonija, 1971). Contains over 200 Greek documents (in the original and in Macedonian translation) concerning the cooperation of EAM-ELAS with the Yugoslav and Bulgarian resistance.

KKE CC. *'Ακροναυπλία—Διαλέξεις* [Akronavplia—Lectures] (Athens, 1945).

KKE CC. *Κομμουνιστική 'Επιθεώρηση τῆς φασιστικῆς κατοχῆς* [The Communist Review of the Fascist Occupation]. (Athens, 1946). Essential source.

KKE. *Σαράντα χρόνια τοῦ KKE, 1918–1958* [40 Years of KKE, 1918–1958] (n.p., 1958).

KKE (Interior). *KKE, 'Επίσημα Κείμενα. Τό Κομμουνιστικό Κόμμα 'Ελλάδας στόν Πόλεμο καί στήν 'Αντίσταση* [KKE Official Texts. The Communist Party of Greece during War and Occupation] Vol. V: 1940–1945, Edited by Alekos Papapanagiotou (n.p. [=Skopje and Rome], 1973).

KKE-KOA. *Λογοδοσία τῆς ἐπιτροπῆς πόλης τῆς ΚΟΑ ἀπό τήν 5η Συνδιάσκεψη ('Απρίλης 1944) μέχρι σήμερα* [Account of the KOA City Committee Activities from the 5th Conference (April 1944) until today] (Athens, 1945).

Kladakes, Markos. "'Έκθεσις 1.6.1944" [Report of 1 June 1944]. In Tsouderos, E.J. *'Επισιτισμός 1941–44. Μέση 'Ανατολή* [Provisioning 1941–44. The Middle East] (Athens, 1948), 41–50. Deals with the antecedents to, and the first phase of, the April 1944 mutiny.

Kouvaras, Costas. *O.S.S. μέ τήν Κεντρική τοῦ E.A.M. 'Αμερικανική μυστική ἀποστολή Περικλής στήν κατεχόμενη 'Ελλάδα* [O.S.S. with the EAM CC. The American Secret Mission Pericles in Occupied Greece] (Athens: Exantas, 1976). The mission leader's diary, 30 April 1944–10 July 1945.

Malvezzi, Piero and Pirelli, Giovanni, eds. *Und die Flamme soll euch nicht versengen. (Letzte Briefe zum Tode Verurteilter aus dem europäischen Widerstand)* (Zurich, 1955).

Marcantonatos, L.G. *A Athènes pendant la guerre. Journal d'un témoin (Octobre 1940–Avril 1944)* (Thessaloniki, Institute for Balkan Studies, 1976).

Megalides, Demetres E. *Λεύκωμα τοῦ ἀγώνα. (ΕΑΜ-ΕΛΑΣ 1941–1945)* [Album of the Struggle (EAM-ELAS 1941–1945)] (Athens, 1946) Contains author's portraits of outstanding representatives of the resistance.

Meletzes, Spyros. *Μέ τούς ἀντάρτες στά βουνά* [With the Guerrillas in the Mountains] (Athens: Meletzes-Papadakes, 1976). About 300 excellent pictures (and some reminiscences) by the "guerrilla photographer."

Milliex, Roger, ed. *Hommage à la Grece 1940–1944. Textes et témoignages français recueillis et présentés par Roger Milliex* (Athens, Institute Français, 1979).

National Bank of Greece. *Reports for the Years 1941–1945* (Athens, 1946).

Papademetriou, Elle *et al.*, eds. *'Εθνική ἀντίσταση 1941–1944. Γράμματα καί μηνύματα ἐκτελεσμένων πατριωτῶν.* [National Resistance 1941–1944. Letters and Messages of Executed Patriots] (Athens: Kedros, 1974).

Papaioannou, Evangelos. "'Η δημοτική ἐκπαίδευσις ἐπί 'Ιταλοκρατίας" [Primary Education under Italian Rule] *Kerkyraika Nea,* 4.7.–22.8.49. Report by the inspector responsible for primary schools in Corfu, submitted to the Ministry of Education.

Paraschos, Costas. *'Η κατοχή. Φωτογραφικά τεκμήρια, 1941–1944* [The Occupation. Photographic Testimonial, 1941–1944] (Athens: Hermes, 1973).

Peniatoglou, L. *'Ελληνικά Προβλήματα* [Greek Problems] (Athens, 1945).

Petimezas, Herakles. "Τά μυστικά τοῦ Νικίτα. Πῶς καί ἀπό ποιούς προδόθηκε ἡ ἀντίσταση." [Nikita's Secrets. How and by Whom the Resistance Was Betrayed] *Akropolis,* 10.6.79 ff. Contains hundreds of letters by Zervas, Psarros, Kartales, Papandreou, and others, including the author.

Pipides, Ioannes D. "'Έκθεσις ἐπί τῶν γεγονότων τῆς 6ης 'Ιουλίου 1943 εἰς 'Ελλ. Ταξιαρχίαν ἐν Ρας-Μπαλπεκ

Συρίας" [Report on the Events of 6 July 1943, in the 2nd Greek Brigade in Ras Baalbek, Syria], *Chiake Epitheoresis,* XIII: 38 (1975), 122–125. Report by the Greek government's Legal Officer, written in August 1943.

"Πρακτικά τῆς Συσκέψεως Μυροφύλλου-Πλάκας" [Minutes of the Conference in Myrophyllo-Plaka], *Historikon Archeion Ethnikes Antistaseos,* 17–19 (1960), 26–100.

Sepheres, Giorgos. *Μέρες.Δ΄ (1 Γενάρη 1941–31 Δεκέμβρη 1944* [Days. Vol. IV. 1 January 1941–31 December 1944] (Athens: Ikaros, 1977).

———. *Πολιτικό Ἡμερολόγιο. Α',* *1935–1944.* [Political Diary. I, 1935–1944] (Athens: Ikaros, 1979).

Τραγούδια τῆς 'Αντίστασης [Songs of the Resistance]. Preface by Costas Varnales (Athens, 1946).

Τραγούδια τῆς ἀντίστασης καί τοῦ ἐμφύλιου: Ε.Α.Μ.—Ε.Λ.Α.Σ.—Ε.Δ.Ε.Σ. 'Εθνικιστικές 'Οργανώσεις [Songs of the Resistance and of the Civil War: EAM—ELAS—EDES. Nationalist Organizations] (Athens: Hellenika Themata, 1975).

Τραγούδια τῆς 'Εθνικῆς 'Αντίστασης [Songs of the National Resistance]. Preface by C. Kophiniotes (Athens, 1945).

Trapeza Ellados [Bank of Greece] Corfu Branch Office. "Δραχμή καί κίνησις κεφαλαίων ἐπί 'Ιταλοκρατίας." [The Drachma and Movement of Capital under Italian Rule] *Kerkyraika Nea,* 19.3.51.

———. "'Η Κέρκυρα τόν Δεκέμβριον τοῦ 1943" [Corfu in December 1943] *Kerkyraika Nea,* 15.–29.12.52. Reports on the economic situation in the island, delivered to the Office of the Governor of the Bank of Greece (April 1943 and 24.12.43).

Voulgares, Petros. "'Η ἐπίσημος ἔκθεσις διά τήν κομμουνιστικήν ἀνταρσίαν τοῦ ἑλληνικοῦ στόλου εἰς τήν Μέσην 'Ανατολήν τήν ἄνοιξιν τοῦ 1944" [The Official Report Concerning the Communist Mutiny in the Greek Middle East Fleet in the spring of 1944], *Akropolis,* 4.4.–27.5.54.

Vovolines, Const. A. *Μυστικές ἐκδόσεις* [Clandestine editions] (Athens, 1945).

Zevgos, Yiannes. "'Ημερολόγιο, 31 *Αὐγούστου–18 'Οκτωβρίου* 1944" [Diary, 31 August–18 October 1944] In Partsalides, M., *Διπλή ἀποκατάσταση . . .* (*infra:*III), 234–242.

C. SOURCES OF NON-GREEK PROVENANCE (RECORDS, MANUALS, DIARIES, CORRESPONDENCE)

Abwehr: "Abwehrstelle III/IIIF, No. 493/43 gKdos., 12.5.1943," *Deutsches Soldatenjahrbuch,* 1971, 275–277. Top secret "Abwehr" report on the tricky seizure of the British commando "Locksmith" (planning the sabotage of the Corinth Canal).

Akten zur Deutschen Auswärtigen Politik. Series "D" and "E". (Göttingen, 1969–1975). English edition: *Documents on German Foreign Policy* (London: HMSO, 1956 ff.).

Bulgaria. Foreign Ministry. *The Truth about the Greek Reparation Claims against Bulgaria* (Sofia, 1946).

Chandler, A.D., ed. *The Papers of Dwight David Eisenhower: The War Years.* 5 vols. (Baltimore and London, 1970).

Ciano, Galeazzo. *Tagebücher 1939–1943* (Bern, 1946). English edition of the *Diary* (New York, 1946).

Comité International de la Croix-Rouge. *Secours à la Grèce 1941–1943.* Typewritten—mimeographed. (Geneva, n.d. [=1944]).

Der Prozess gegen die Hauptkriegsverbrecher vor dem Internationalen Militärgerichtshof. (Nuremberg, 1947–1949). English edition: *The Trial of Major War Criminals* (Nuremberg, 1947–1949). Scattered references to Greece.

Dilks, David, ed. *Sir Alexander Cadogan. The Diaries 1938–1945.* (New York, 1972). Much insider's information on British policy-making with respect to Greece by Britain's Permanent Under-Secretary of State.

Documents Regarding the Situation in Greece. January 1945. (London: HMSO, 1945). Most documents refer to the December events. Included in the collection, however, is the Political Charter of EDES, purged of all anti-Monarchist statements contained in the original text.

Domarus, Max, ed. *Adolf Hitler. Reden und Proklamationen, 1932–1945.* Vol. II. (Würzburg, 1963).

Georgieff, P. and Spiru, B., eds. *Bulgariens Volk im Widerstand (1941–1944* ([East-] Berlin, 1962). Some of the documents refer to the collaboration of Bulgarian anti-Fascists with KKE/EAM/ELAS.

Great Britain. Foreign Office. *Greece. Basic Handbook.* Restricted. (London, 1943).

———. *Greece. Zone Handbooks.* Restricted. (London, 1943/44).

———. Parliament. *Parliamentary Debates* (House of Commons), 5th series. 1941–44.

Heiber, Helmut, ed. *Hitlers Lagebesprechungen. Die Protokollfragmente seiner militärischen Konferenzen 1942–1945* (Stuttgart, 1962).

Helger, Bengt, ed. *Rapport final de la Commission de Gestion pour les Secours en Grèce sous les auspices du Comité International de la Croix Rouge. Ravitaillement de la Grèce pendant l'occupation 1941–1944 et pendant les premiers cinq mois après la liberation* (Athens, 1949).

Hillgruber, Andreas, ed. *Staatsmänner und Diplomaten bei Hitler. Vertrauliche Aufzeichnungen.* 2 vols. (Frankfurt, 1967/70). Several of the talks (especially with Italian or Bulgarian politicians) also refer to Greece (strategy, occupation problems, post-war aspirations, general views).

Hubatsch, Walther, ed. *Hitlers Weisungen für die Kriegsführung 1939–1945* (Frankfurt, 1962).

Italy. Ministero della Difesa. Stato Maggiore dell' Esercito, Ufficio Storico. *Bolletini di Guerra del Comando Supremo 1940–1943* (Roma, 1970).

Moran, Lord. *Winston Churchill: The Struggle for Survival 1940–1965* (London, 1966). The Diaries of Churchill's private physician contain some valuable first-hand accounts on the prime minister's policy for Greece.

Muggeridge, M., ed. *Ciano's Diplomatic Papers* (London, 1948).

Murawski, Erich, ed. *Der deutsche Wehrmachtsbericht 1939–1945* (Boppard, 1962).

Papakongos, Costas, ed. *'Αρχεῖο Πέρσον. Κατοχικά ντοκουμέντα τοῦ Δ.Ε.Σ. Πελοποννήσου* [The Persson Archive. Documents of the International Red Cross in the Peloponnesus. Occupation Years] (Athens: Papazeses, 1977).

Picker, Henry and Schramm, Percy Ernst, eds. *Hitlers Tischgespräche im Führerhauptquartier 1941–42* (Stuttgart, 1963).

Schramm, Percy Ernst, ed. *Kriegstagebuch des Oberkommandos der Wehrmacht.* 4 vols. (Frankfurt, 1961–1965). Essential source.

U.S. Army Service Forces, Headquarters. *Civil Affairs Handbook. GREECE. Manual M 351.* Restricted. (Washington, D.C., December 1943).

———. Board of Economic Warfare (Blockade and Supply Branch, Reoccupation Division). *Key Laws, Decrees and Regulations Issued by the Axis in Occupied Europe: Greece* (Washington, D.C., June 1943)

———. Department of State. *Foreign Relations of the United States.* Diplomatic Papers 1941; vol. II; 1942, vol. III; 1943, vol. IV; 1944, vol.V. (Washington, D.C.: Government Printing Office, 1959–1965). Essential source.

———. Foreign Economic Administration. *A Survey of Greek Relief, April 1941 to December 1943.* In collaboration with the State Department. Restricted. (Washington, D.C, March 1944).

———. *A Summary of Greek Internal Politics 1941–1946 (For the Use of the United States Mission to Observe the Greek Elections).* Secret. (n.p., January 1946).

U.S.S.R. Ministry of Foreign Affairs. *Correspondence between the Chairman of the Council of Ministers of the USSR, the Presidents of the USA and the Prime Ministers of Great Britain during the Great Patriotic War of 1941–1945* (London, 1958).

Vatican. Secrétairerie d' Etat de sa Sainteté. *Actes et documents du Saint Siège Relatifs à la Seconde Guerre Mondiale.* Vols. IV, V, VII, VIII, (Città del Vaticano, 1967–1974). Contains many scattered references to Greece, in particular exchanges of notes on the relief problem, and many informative memoranda, etc., by A.G. Roncalli (the subsequent Johannes XXIII), nuncio for Turkey and Greece.

Wagner, Gerhard, ed. *Lagevorträge des Oberbefehlshabers der Kriegsmarine vor Hitler 1939–1945* (Munich, 1972).

Willis, Algernon U. "Naval Operations in the Aegean between the 7th September, 1943 and 28th November, 1943." (Despatch submitted to the Lords Commissioners of the Admiralty on the 27th December, 1943). *Supplement to the London Gazette,* 38426 (October 1948), 5371–5379.

Wilson, H. Maitland. "Operations in the Middle East from 16th February, 1943, to 8th January, 1944" (Despatch submitted to the Secretary of State for War on 31st August, 1944). *Supplement to the London Gazette,* 37786 (November 1946), 5569–5604.

Works of Art in Greece, the Greek Islands and the Dodecanese. Losses and Survivals in the War (London: HMSO, 1946).

Yugoslavia. Office of Information. *Book on Greece* (Beograd, 1948). The official answer to Greek "monarchofascist" charges at the United Nations concerning Yugoslav support of "Democratic Army" guerrillas. Some references to the occupation period.

Zöllner, M. and Leszczynski, K., eds. *Fall 7. Das Urteil im Geiselmordprozess. (Gefällt am 19.2.1948 vom Militärgerichtshof V der USA)* ([East-] Berlin, 1965). The verdict of the American Military Tribunal in the case against the leading German generals acting in South East Europe during the war years. Commentary by M. Zöllner.

D. WARTIME PUBLICATIONS OTHER THAN GREEK CLANDESTINE ISSUES

Amyntor. *Victors in Chains* (London: Greek Information Office, n.d.).

Angelopoulos, Angelos Th. *'Ο σοσιαλισμός* [Socialism] (Athens, 1944).

Anglo-Hellenic League. *Greece and Her Fight for Freedom* (London, n.d., =1941)

Archer, Laird. *Balkan Journal* (New York, 1944). The director of the Near East Foundation gives a vivid account of life in Athens during the Albanian campaign and the early period of the occupation.

Bachmann, Franz. "Der Einfluss des Judentums in Griechenland," *Volk im Osten* (Bucharest), IV: 5–6 (1943), 56–62.

Bathe, Rolf and Glodschey, Erich. *Der Kampf um den Balkan* (Oldenburg and Berlin, 1942).

Bistes, Panteles G. *'Ηχώ ἀπό τό Λονδίνο* [Echo from London] (Cyprus, 1944). The author's commentaries on BBC and talks broadcast to Cyprus, 7.2.43–18.2.44.

Busch-Zantner, Richard. *Bulgarien.* 2nd ed. (Leipzig, 1943).

———. "Das griechisch-albanische Grenzproblem," *Wir und die Welt,* III (1941), 33–36.

Capidan, Th. *Die Mazedorumänen* (Bucharest, 1941).

———. "Darstellung der ethnologischen Lage am Balkan mit besonderer Berücksichtigung der Mazedorumänen (Aromunen)," *Südostforschungen,* VII (1942), 497–545. The author deals with the history of the Balkan Vlachs and with their "oppression" by the majority nations. Calls for German intervention.

Capps, Edward. *Greece, Albania and Northern Epirus* (New York, n.d.). Ex-ambassador in Athens supports Greek aspirations.

Casson, Stanley. *Greece against the Axis.* 2nd ed. (Washington, D.C., 1943).

Chrysochoou, Athanasios. *'Εγκύκλιος Λαϊκῆς Διαφωτίσεως* [Encyclical for People's Enlightenment] (Thessaloniki, April 1943). One of the many vehemently anti-EAM (but also cautiously anti-Bulgarian) brochures written by the Governor-General of Macedonia and circulated among Greek officials. Copies were sent to the German authorities as well as to the Greek Government-in-exile and to the British secret services.

C.M.C. "Bulgaria and the War." *Bulletin of International News,* 13.11.43, 991–994 and 27.11.43, 1031–1039.

Cockburn, Claude. [= Pitcairn, Frank]. "The Truth about Greece". *Daily Worker,* 20.3.44.

David, Ben, ed. *Greece is our Concern* (London: London School of Economics, Socialist Society and University Labour Federation, 1945).

Davis, Homer. *Greece Fights: The People Behind the Front* (New York, 1942). Account by the president of Athens College.

Demades, C. "'Η Θεσσαλονίκη χθές καί σήμερον." [Thessaloniki, Yesterday and Today] *Athenaika Nea* 12.–14.6.41.

———. "'Η σημερινή κατάστασις είς τήν Θεσσαλονίκην" [Today's Situation in Thessaloniki] *Athenaika Nea,* 8.8.41.

Democritus League. *Greek Liberation: EAM—the Liberation Movement in Greece* (Melbourne, 1944).

"Die Tätigkeit der Degriges." *Südost-Economist* (Budapest), 10.12.43. Refers to the Deutsch-Griechische Warenausgleichs-Gesellschaft, founded in order to secure minimum continuation of Greek-German trade, thereby reducing Germany's occupation costs.

Dobransky, Rudolf. "Der Erzbergbau in Griechenland." *Metall und Erz* (Halle), XXXIX: V/VI (1942), 89–92, 111–113.

E.E. (*'Ελληνόφιλος Ἕλλην*) [Philehellene Greek] "Quo vadis Grecia; . . . *καί ὀλίγη ἱστορία*" [Quo Vadis Grecia? . . . and a Little History] *Akropolis,* 10.–11.3.44.

Eckert, Erhardt. *Südöstliche Reise. Auf den Siegesstrassen durch den befriedeten Balkan* (Berlin, 1943).

EEE (*'Εθνική Ἕνωσις 'Ελλάδος*) [National Union of Greece] "'Ημεῖς καί οἱ ἄλλοι" [We and the Others] *Akropolis,* 5.–7-4-44.

Fels, E. "Griechenlands wirtschaftliche und politische Lage." *Geographische Zeitschrift,* XXXXVII (1941/2), 57–71.

"Flugblattkrieg der griechischen Partisanen." *Neue Ordnung* (Zagreb), (23.1.44), 7.

Gkotzamanes, Soterios. *Τό μακεδονικόν ζήτημα. ('Αγών κατά τῆς αὐτονομήσεως)* [The Macedonian Issue. (Struggle against Autonomy)] 2nd ed. (Athens, 1943). Reprint of the 1912 edition, by the collaborationist minister of economy.

v. Golitschek, Josef. "Bandenkrieg der Rivalen." *Das Reich,* 6.8.44.

———. "Griechenland und die Briten." *Leipziger Neueste Nachrichten,* 19.12.44.

———. "Griechenland auf Neuen Wegen." *Leipziger Neueste Nachrichten,* 30.5.44.

Greece. Government Office of Information. *Ruins of Modern Greece. Cities and Villages of Greece Destroyed by Germans, Italians and Bulgars, 1941–1944* (Washington, D.C, n.d. [= 1944]).

Greece. Hellenike Hyperesia Typou [Greek Press Service]. *Οἱ Βούλγαροι στή Μακεδονία* [The Bulgars in Macedonia] (Cairo, 1944).

———. *'Η Σύσκεψις τοῦ Λιβάνου. 'Εκεῖ πού συνετάγη τό 'Ελληνικό 'Εθνικό Συμβούλιο* [The Lebanon Conference. Where the Greek National Charter Was Drawn Up] (Cairo, 1944).

———. Hyperesia Plerophorion [Information Service] *Εἰδικόν Δελτίον* 28.10.43 [Special Bulletin, 28.10,43] (Washington, D.C., 1943). Deals with Greek resistance and German reprisals.

Greece. Information Department. *Le Drame des Juifs Hellénes* (Cairo, 1944).

———. Office of Information. *Greece Undaunted still Fights on. Speeches and Addresses by His Majesty King George II of the Hellenes in the United States of America and the Dominion of Canada, June—July 1942* (New York, n.d. [= 1942]).

———. Office of Information. *Facts About Fighting Greece* (Washington, D.C., n.d.).

———. Office of Information. *Greece in Arms* (London, 1944).

Greek-American Labor Committee, ed. *Greece Fights for Freedom* (New York, January 1944).

Greek Unity Committee. *The Truth about Greece* (London, n.d. [= 1944]).

"Griechenland im Neuen Werden." *Neue Ordnung* I: 40 (1942), 4.

"Griechenland in der Zeitenwende." *Neue Ordnung,* III: 125–126 (1943/44), 6.

"Griechenland unter Umstellungszwang." *Berliner Börsenzeitung,* 10.8.41.

"Griechinnen in Kriegszeit." *Strassburger Neueste Nachrichten,* 21.1.44.

"Griechische Besinnung." *Neue Ordnung,* II: 65 (1942), 13.

"Griechische Probleme." *Berliner Börsenzeitung,* 10.9.41.

Grünwald, Rolf. *Südosteuropa als Absatzmarkt für Konsumfertigwaren.* (Vienna: Südosteuropa-Gesellschaft, 1944).

v. Hassell, [Ulrich]. "Deutschlands wirtschaftliche Interessen und Aufgaben in Südosteuropa." *Zeitschrift für Politik,* XXXI (1941), 481–488. Similarly:

———. "Die Neuordung in Südosteuropa." *Berliner Monatshefte,* XIX (1941), 601–611.

Holler, Ernst. "Aus Feldpostbriefen über Griechenland." *Deutsche Höhere Schule,* X:3 (1943), 86–93. Letters containing impressions from German soldiers in Greece.

Hourmouzios, S.L. *Starvation in Greece* (London, 1943). Largely pictorial.

Hünger, Heinz and Strassl, Ernst E. *Kampf und Intrige um Griechenland* (Munich, 1942).

Illyricus. *Greece and Albania* (London, 1944). A pro-Albanian pamphlet referring to the Northern Epirus dispute and to Greek aspirations.

Inter-Allied Information Committee. *Conditions in Occupied Territories.* 1. *The Axis System of Hostages* (19.3.42). 2. *Rationing Under Axis Rule* (4.5.42). (London: HMSO, 1942). (Presumably, additional brochures were issued).

Justice for Greece Committee. *The Hellenic Character of Northern Epirus* (London and Washington, D.C., n.d.).

Kaklamanos, Demetrios. *Γύρω ἀπό τόν πόλεμο* [About the War] (Cairo, 1942).

Kanellopoulos, Panagiotes. *'Η 'Ελλάς καί ὁ πόλεμος* [Greece and the War] (Cairo, 1942).

———. *Τί ὀφείλει στήν 'Ελλάδα ἡ Διεθνής Δικαιοσύνη* [What International Justice Owes Greece] (Alexandria, 1944).

Karamanos, Georgios J. ed. *Lest we Forget that Noble and Immortal Nation . . . Greece* (New York, 1943).

Karlic, D. "Nationale Selbstbesinnung in Griechenland." *Neue Ordnung,* 2.7.44, 5.

Kästner, Erhart. *Griechenland—ein Buch aus dem Kriege* (Berlin, 1943).

Katsilambros, D. "'Ο Ἕλλην κυβερνήτης: *'Ο Γ. Τσολάκογλου καί ἡ ἱστορία τῆς αὔριον*" [The Greek Ruler: G. Tsolakoglou and the History of Tomorrow], *He Kathemerine* 23.12.41.

Kent, Ralph. "I Saw Greece Looted." *The Nation,* 16.8.1941, 136–138.

Kohler, Foy D. "The Relief of Occupied Greece.' *Department of State Bulletin,* 17.9.44, 300–305.

Kondakes, Andreas D. "Νέες κατευθύνσεις εἰς τήν ἐργασίαν." [New Directions in Labor], *Akropolis,* 4.–7.11.41.

Koromelas, Lambros G. *33 ἄρθρα γιά τόν στρατό, τόν στόλο, τήν ἀεροπορία, τούς κομμάντος μας* [33 Articles on our Army, our Navy, our Air Force, our Commando Units] (Cairo, 1945). Articles from Greek newspapers in Middle East, 1942–1944.

Kotzias, Costas G. *'Ελλάς. 'Ο πόλεμος καί ἡ δόξα της* [Greece. The War and Her Glory] (New York, 1943).

Koutsoumes, Dinos. *Εἰκόνες τῆς Γερμανοκρατούμενης 'Ελλάδος* [Pictures from German-Occupied Greece] (Alexandria, 1942).

Krohm, Hartmut. *Die Textilindustrie Südosteuropas* (Prague and Vienna: Südosteuropa-Gesellschaft, 1944).

Kulischer, Eugene M. *The Displacement of Population in Europe* (Montreal, 1943).

Lavra, Stephen. *The Greek Miracle* (New York, 1943).
"Lebendige Wirklichkeit in Griechenland." *Neue Ordnung,* III: 115 (1943–44), 6.
Leibrock, Otto. *Der Südosten, Grossdeutschland und das neue Europa* (Berlin, 1941).
Lemkin, Raphael. *Axis Rule in Occupied Europe* (Washington, 1944).
Levy, Raphael, *La Tragedia de los Tzidios en los Balcanes* (Istanbul, 1942).
Logothetopoulos, Constantine. "*Ἡ πρόνοια δέν εἶναι ἐλεημοσύνη.*" [Providence is not Charity] *He Kathemerine,* 13.11.41.
Lourantos, Georgios E. *Εἷς οἰωνός ἄριστος ἀμύνεσθαι περί πάτρης* [The Best Augury is the Defense of the Fatherland] (Alexandria, 1942)
Lucas, Walter. "In Greece 'Quislings' are pro-British." *Daily Express,* 11.10.44.
Mackenzie, Compton. *Wind of Freedom* (London, 1943).
Marinos, Charalambos D. "Πῶς πρέπει νά τρέφεται σήμερον ὁ 'Ελληνικός λαός" [How the Greek People Should Be Nourished Today], *He Kathemerine,* 19.12.41.
Marketos, Babes. *'Η 'Ελλάς στό σταυροδρόμι* [Greece at the Crossroad] (New York, 1942).
Markou, M. A. *Κάμνομεν πόλεμον* [We Make War] (Cairo, 1942).
———. *'Η 'Ελλάς δέν ἡττήθη* [Greece Has Not Been Defeated] (Cairo, 1943).
M.E.P. "Greece and the War." *Bull. of International News,* 5.2.44, 91–101 and 19.2.44, 135–144.
Michalopoulos, André. *Greek Fire* (London, 1943). Contains a selection of broadcasts and other speeches dedicated to the Albanian campaign and the resistance.
Monasteriotes, Petros. *Οἱ Πρῶσσοι τῶν Βαλκανίων* [The Prussians of the Balkans] (Cairo, 1944).
Müller, Günther and Scheuering, Fritz. *Sprung über Kreta* (Oldenburg, 1944).
Neubacher, Hermann. "Kein Neuer Balkanbund." *Donau-Zeitung* (Belgrade), 3.11.43. (Interview).
Nikoulakos, P. N. *Οἱ Βούλγαροι, οἱ αἱμοβορώτεροι ἄνθρωποι, οἱ ἀσπονδότεροι ἐχθροί μας* [The Bulgars, the Most Bloodthirsty Men, Our Most Relentless Enemies] (Alexandria, 1944).
Ntangras, K. "Βλέμματα στήν 'Ελληνική ἐπαρχία." [Glances at the Greek Province] *Athenaika Nea,* 16.–19.7., 24.–25.7., 29.–30.7.,9.8.41. Refers to Thessaly.
Olshausen, Franz. "Ein Jahr später. Belgrad und Athen, April 1941." *Berliner Monatshefte,* XX: 5 (May 1942), 227–233.
Paneth, Philip. *The Glory That Is Greece* (London, n.d.).
Papandreou, Georgios. *'Ο λόγος τῆς ἀπελευθερώσεως.* [The Speech of Liberation, 18 October 1944] (Athens, n.d. [=1944]) R
Pappamikail, Emmanouel Th. *Grēcia: A Contribuicão da Grēcia.* (Lisbon, n.d. [=1943]).
Parisius, Dr. "Die griechische Statts- und Selbstverwaltung und die deutsche Militärverwaltung in Griechenland." *Reichsverwaltungsblatt,* LXIII: 7/8 (19.2.42), 61–64.
———. "Die griechischen Gemeinden vor und nach dem Einmarsch der deutschen Truppen." *Der Gemeindetag,* XXXVI: 15/16 (August 1942), 181–182.
Patitsas, Philemon. "Griechenlands europäische Aufgabe." *Die deutsche Volkswirtschaft,* XI: 36 (1942), 1403–1406.

Pipinelis, M. P. *Caitiff Bulgaria* (London: by authority of the Greek Ministry of Information, n.d.).

———. *Such Are the Bulgars* (London, n.d.).

Pistolakis, Stelios. *The Truth about Greece* (New York: Greek-American Committee for National Unity, September, 1944).

———. "Πώς ή 'Αγγλία επρόδωσε τήν 'Ελλάδα καί τήν παρέδωσε στά χέρια τής πείνας" [How England Betrayed Greece and Handed Her over into the Claws of Starvation] *He Kathemerine* 24.12.41; nearly identical: *Athenaika Nea* 24.12.41.

Potamianos, Ch. *'Οκτώ ραδιοφωνικαί ὁμιλίαι τοῦ Ἕλληνος Στρατιώτου. 'Η 'Ελλας ἀκούει* [Eight Broadcasts of the Greek Soldier. Greece Is Listening] (Cairo, 1943).

Puscariu, Sextil. "Die Rumänen auf dem Balkan." *Berliner Monatshefte,* XIX: 6 (1941), 406–415.

Reutersward, Pontus. *Greklands Krig 1940–41* (Stockholm, 1943).

Rodinus, P. *The Fight in Greece* (London, 1943).

Ronneberger, Franz. "Griechenland—Schicksal und Verschulden." *Zeitschrift für Politik,* XXXI: 5 (1941), 267–276.

Saint-John, Robert. *From the Land of Silent People* (Garden City, N.Y., 1942).

Schumacher, Hans. "Griechenland." *Volk im Osten,* IV: 10–12 (1943), 87–89, 110–113.

Student, [Kurt], ed. *Kreta, Sieg der Kühsten. Von Heldenkampf der Fallschirmjager* (Graz, 1942).

Südosteuropa-Gesellschaft. *Der italienische Einfluss auf die Industriewirtschaft in Südosteuropa seit Kriegsbeginn.* Typewritten—mimeographed, restricted (Geheim). (Vienna, 1943).

———. *Die Bodenschätze der südosteuropäischen Länder.* 2 vols. Restricted (Streng vertraulich). (Vienna, 1943/44).

———. *Die südosteuropäischen Eisenbahnen* (Vienna, 1942).

———. Compare also: Grünwald, Krohm.

Symmachos. *Greece Fights On* (London, n.d. [=1943]).

The Greek White Book. (Diplomatic Documents Relating to Italy's Aggression against Greece. With a preface by Emmanuel Tsouderos, (pp. 5–18). 2nd enlarged ed. (Washington, D.C., 1943).

The National Committee for the Restoration of Greece. *Greece under Nazi and Fascist Rule* (New York, 1941).

Tsolakoglou, Georgios. "Ἅμιλλα εἰς θυσίας, σιδηρά πειθαρχία καί γρανιτώδης πίστις ἐπί τό μέλλον τοῦ ἔθνους, ἰδοῦ τί δύναται νά σώση τήν 'Ελλάδα." [Sacrifices, Iron Discipline and Granite-like Belief in the Nation's Future: That is what can Save Greece] *Athenaika Nea,* 17.10.41.

Tsouderos, Emmanuel J. *Democracy or Monocracy? Why We Are Fighting.* (Washington, D.C., n.d. [=1941]).

———. *The Greek Epic* (London, n.d.[=1942]).

———. *Greek White Paper. Axis Crimes in Greece.* (Memorandum submitted by the Prime Minister of Greece at the Inter-Allied Conference at St. James's Palace, on January 13th, 1942, and addressed to all Allied and Friendly Governments) (London, 1942).

———. *Δύο ὁμιλίες τοῦ Ἕλληνος Πρωθυπουργοῦ* [Two Speeches by the Greek Prime Minister] (Alexandria, 1942).

———. *Λόγοι ἑνός χρόνου* [Speeches of One Year] (Alexandria, 1942).

"Unter der Akropolis." *Frankfurter Zeitung* (Reichsausgabe), 15.11.42.

v. Uzorinac, Teodor. "Hellas am Scheidewege." *Neue Ordnung*, III: 116 (24.10.43), 1–2.

"Vernarbende Wunden. Griechenland nach einem Jahr." *Das Reich*, 26.10.42, 4.

Wason, Betty. *Miracle in Hellas. The Greeks Fight On* (London, 1943).

Weber, Hans Adolf. "Festung Kreta—eine feuerspeiende Insel." *Leipziger Neueste Nachrichten*, 27.7.43.

"Westthrazien und Südmazedonien in der bulgarischen Wirtschaft." *Südost-Economist* 6.6.41, 203–204.

White, Leigh. *The Long Balkan Night* (New York, 1944).

Wirsing, Giselher. *Der Krieg 1939/41 in Karten* (Munich, 1942).

Xydis, Stephen G. *The Economy and Finances of Greece under Occupation* (New York: Greek Govt. Office of Information, 1944).

III. Published Secondary Sources

(Memoirs and Secondary Literature)

Abendroth, Wolfgang. *Ein Leben in der Arbeiterbewegung*. B. Dietrich and J. Perels, eds. (Frankfurt/M.: Suhrkamp, 1976). /1,5,7,L/ This collection of interviews contains some pages on the cooperation of German antifascists with EAM.

Adamos, Takes. "'Από τή δράση τοῦ ἀρχηγείου τοῦ ΕΛΑΣ Σουλίου-'Ηπείρου" [Activities of the ELAS Detachment of Souli-Epirus], *Ethnike Antistase,* 4 (April 1963), 361–370; 5 (August 1963), 478–488. / 2,6,L/

———. "Τό ΚΚΕ καί ἡ 'Εθνική 'Αντίσταση" [The KKE and the National Resistance], *Kommounistike Epitheorese,* April 1975, 7–14.

———. *Τό λαϊκό τραγοῦδι τῆς ἀντίστασης.* [The Popular Song of the Resistance], 2nd enlarged edition (Athens: Kastaniotes, 1977). /L/ Contains the bulk of resistance songs as well as a useful evaluation of this form of expression.

Agapetides, S. and Pizanias, N. *Τό κόστος τῆς στοιχειώδους συντηρήσεως κατά τήν κατοχήν* [The Cost of Basic Sustenance during the Occupation] (Athens, 1945).

Agapetos, Angelakes. *Σκέψεις καί ἐντυπώσεις ἀπό τόν 'Ελληνικόν ἀγῶνα. (Στήν 'Ελλάδα καί Μ. 'Ανατολή* [Thoughts and Impressions from the Greek Struggle. (In Greece and in the Middle East)]. (Middle East Concentration Camps. 1944–45). / 1,4,5,L / An excellent left-wing report of intra-Greek frictions in Macedonia and Egypt; provides much insider's information on the mutiny in April 1944.

Akritakis, Akis. "Komunistyczna Partija Grecji a Grecki riuch oporu w iatach 1941–1945" [The Communist Party of Greece and the Greek Resistance Movement 1941–1945] *Z Pola Walki* (Poland), XVIII: 70 (1975), 67–91. Not consulted.

Alexandres, C.A. *Τό ναυτικόν μας κατά τήν πολεμικήν περίοδον 1941–45* [Our Navy during the War Period 1941–45] (Athens, 1952). / 4,6 / A valuable account by the former fleet commander (1943–44), but not free from errors apparently dictated by considerations of self-defense.

Alexiou, Elle. "Νά ἕνας σωστός Ἕλληνας! 'Ο Κοτζιούλας καί τό θέατρό του στά βουνά" [Here is a True Greek! Kotzioulas and His Theatre in the Mountains], *Theatro,* 9: 53–54 (1976), 57–60. Reminiscences of the guerrilla playwright Kotzioulas and short reviews of his extant plays.

Anagnostopoulos, Nikolaos Ath. *'Η Εὔβοια ὑπό κατοχήν* [Euboea Occupied]. 2 vols. (Athens, 1950, 1973). /2,3,6,R / A defense of the collaborating Security Battalions, which provides ample pertinent material as well as many announcements by the occupation authorities. However, on specific points the narrative should be used with utmost caution.

Andreou, Nikos, ed. *'Εθνική 'Αντίσταση, τό ἔπος τοῦ λαοῦ.* [National Resistance, the People's Epic] (Athens: Synchrone Epoche, 1975). /1,2,3,6,L/ Contains some documents as well as articles and reminiscences by various authors, dealing with the resistance and reprisals.

Andrews, Kevin. *The Flight of Ikaros. A Journey into Greece* (London, 1959). /2,3,6,7 / Much informative (but sometimes wrong) hearsay evidence concerning ELAS and the Security Battalions.

Andrikopoulos, Yiannes. *1944, κρίσιμη χρονιά* [1944, Critical Year]. 2 vols. (Athens: Diogenes, 1974). Collection of 300 documents concerning Greece from the personal files of W.S. Churchill.

Angelopoulos, Angelos Th. *Τό οἰκονομικό πρόβλημα τῆς 'Ελλάδος* [The Economic Problem of Greece] (Athens, 1945) / 8 /

———, *et al.* "Τά δάνεια τῆς 'Ελλάδος πρός τήν Γερμανία καί τήν 'Ιταλία" [The Greek Loans to Germany and Italy], *Nea Oikonomia,* (1964), 407–414. Deals with the forced loans to the occupation authorities.

Angelopoulos, Ar. "Τά ἀπόρρητα ἀρχεῖα τῆς ἀμερικανικῆς κατασκοπίας εἰς τήν 'Ελλάδα" [The Secret Archives of the American Espionage Service in Greece], *Akropolis,* 16.5.–15.6.54. / 1,2,R /

Angeloules, Antones [Vratsanos]. *Βροντάει ὁ Ὄλυμπος* [Olympus Thunders] (Athens, 1945). / 2,5 / Sweeping account by the famous "train-buster" of ELAS, who seriously damaged German north-south communications.

Antaios, Petros [= St. Yiannakopoulos]. *Συμβολή στήν ἱστορία τῆς ΕΠΟΝ* [Contribution to the History of EPON]. 2 vols. (Athens: Kastaniotes, 1977). / 1,2,6,8,L / Best work on the EAM youth organization.

Antonakeas, Nikos A. *Πῶς εἶδον τόν ἀπελευθερωτικόν ἀγῶνα κατά τά ἔτη 1941–1945* [How I Saw the Liberation Struggle during the Years 1941–1945] (Athens, 1945). / 1,6,R /

———. *Φῶς εἰς τό σκότος τῆς κατοχῆς* [Light into the Darkness of the Occupation] (Athens, 1947). This book is indispensable for the extreme right-wing (royalist) version of resistance history, and also demonstrates the potentialities of polemical distortion.

Antonakos, Sarantos P. "'Η τραγωδία τῶν Καλαβρύτων." [The Tragedy of Kalavryta] *Historia,* 90 (Dec. 1975), 96–103.

Antonopoulos, Kosmas E. *'Εθνική 'Αντίστασις 1941–1945* [National Resistance 1941–45]. 3 vols. (Athens, 1964). / 1,2,6,R / Most of the 1830 pages are filled with fanciful heroics about the patriotic intentions and imaginary successes of nationalist resistance organizations which finally were dissolved by the "treacherous" EAM-ELAS. Author deals primarily with the Peloponnesus, where he was member of a somewhat obscure group.

Antonovski, Hr. "Dramskoto vostanie od 1941 godina i Bulgarksite fašistički zlostorstva" [The Revolt in Drama in 1941 and the Bulgarian Fascist Crimes] *Glasnik,* 1 (1961), 57–74. Greek translation in *Deltio Slavikis Vivliographias,* 17 (1968), 25–43. /2,3,L/.

Apostolou, Lefteres. *Τί ἔκαμε τό EAM γιά τήν 'Ελλάδα* [What EAM Did for Greece] (Athens, 1945). / 1,L /

———. *Ἡ παρωδία τῆς δίκης τῶν δοσιλόγων καί ἡ αὐτοκαταδίκη τῆς δεξιᾶς* [The Parody of the Collaborators' Trial and the Self-Condemnation of the Right] (Athens, 1945). The same work appeared anonymously earlier in 1945, under the title *Ἡ κωμωδία τῆς δίκης τῶν δοσιλόγων.*

———. "Τό ΕΑΜ καί ἡ Ἐθνική Ἀντίσταση τοῦ 1941–44." [EAM and the National Resistance 1941–44], *Avge* 25.9.76.

"Ἄρης Βελουχιώτης. Ἡ ἀνταρτική ἐποποιΐα τοῦ ἔθνους" [Ares Velouchiotes. The Guerrilla Epic of the Nation], *Elefthere Hellada,* 22.6–9.8.45. / 2,6,L/ A group of former "kapetanioi," one of them probably Ph. Gregoriades, composed this remarkably moderate report immediately after Ares' mysterious death.

Argenti, Philip. P. *The Occupation of Chios by the Germans and their Administration of the Island* (Cambridge, 1966). / 1,3,6 / Lengthy appendix contains many German and Greek documents.

Arnold, Theodor. *Der revolutionäre Krieg* (Pfaffenhofen, 1961). A chapter deals with "the first revolutionary war in Greece." Background material.

Arseniou, Laz. A. *Ἡ Θεσσαλία στήν Ἀντίσταση* [Thessaly in the Resistance]. Vol. I. (n.p., 1966); Vol. II (Athens: p.a. press, 1977). / 1,2,6,L / The author, leading member of the Thessalian EAM, has collected many eye-witness reports and samples of the hard-to-find resistance press. His synopsis provides one of the few accounts by a participant which strives for some impartiality. Best source on Thessaly.

Asdrachas, Spyros I. "Μερικές σημειώσεις γιά τά τεκμήρια τῆς Ἑλληνικῆς ἀντίστασης" [Some Notes Concerning the Evidence of the Greek Resistance], *Anti* 4.10.75, 41–45.

Asterinos, Demetrios. "Ἀπό τήν Καζέρτα ἕως τήν ἀπελευθέρωση" [From Caserta to the Liberation], *Historia,* 76 (Oct. 74), 14–18.

Athanassiades, Athanassios P. *Τί ἔκαμα γιά τήν Ἑλλάδα* [What I Did for Greece] (Athens, 1949). / 1,3,5,R / Author was leading member of a counter-intelligence and sabotage group among the police of Athens.

Athanassiades, Georgis. *Ἡ πρώτη πράξη τῆς Ἑλληνικῆς τραγωδίας. Μέση Ἀνατολή 1941–44* [The First Act of the Greek Tragedy. Middle East 1941–44] (Athens: Planetes, 1975). / 4,6,8,L / Author offers good insight into the Greek "antifascist scene" of the Middle East. However, he cites (from secret party documents) only the "suitable" passages and omits those disclosing (local) Communist parentage of the mutinies.

Athenaios, I. "Ἀπό τήν ὀργάνωση καί τή δράση τοῦ ΕΛΑΣ Ἀθήνας-Πειραιᾶ" [On the Organization and Activities of the ELAS of Athens/Piraeus], *Ethnike Antistase,* 2 (Aug. 1962), 118–135. / 1,2,6,L /

"Aus dem Freiheitskampf der Studenten Griechenlands." In K.H. Jahnke, ed., *Niemals Vergessen* (East Berlin, 1959). / 1,6,7,L / Deals with the student resistance, 1941–1944.

Auty, Phyllis and Clogg, Richard, eds. *British Policy towards Wartime Resistance in Yugoslavia and Greece* (London: Macmillan, 1975). Contains informative expositions by Woodhouse, Myers, and various SOE and Foreign Office officials, as well as a series of candid discussions elucidating British inter-agency friction during that period.

Averoff-Tossizza, E. *Le feu et la hâche.—Grèce 1946–1949* (Paris: Breteuil, 1973). Greek edition: *Φωτιά καί τσεκούρι* (Athens: Hestia, 1974). English edition: *By Fire and Axe: The Communist Party and the Civil War in Greece, 1946–49* (New Rochelle: Caratzas, 1978). /1,2,7,R/ The book deals primarily with the civil war, but also provides background material on the occupation years. Contains a number of errors and misinterpretations, particularly as to Communist activities and strategy.

Avgeres, Markos. "'Η ἀντίσταση, δημιουργός νέας ἐθνικῆς συνείδησης" [The Resistance, Creator of a New National Conscience], *Avge* 26.9.76. First published in *Pyrsos* (1964).

Avni, Haim. "Spanish Nationals in Greece and Their Fate during the Holocaust." In *Yad Vashem Studies* 8 (1970), 31–68.

Axiote, Melpo. *Οἱ 'Ελληνίδες—φρουροί τῆς 'Ελλάδας* [Greek Women—Sentinels of Greece] (Athens, 1945). /1,L/ Tribute to some outstanding women in the resistance.

———. *'Αθήνα 1941–1945* [Athens 1941–1945] (Athens, 1945). /1,6,7,L/. Resistance, reprisals, suffering.

Bakalbases, A.G. *'Η οἰκονομία τῆς 'Ελλάδος καί ἡ ὀργανωμένη ἰδιωτική πρωτοβουλία 1941–44* [The Economy of Greece and Organized Private Initiative 1941–44] (Athens, 1944). /6/

———. *A.E. Ella Turk. 'Αναγνώρισις μίας συμβολῆς εἰς τόν ἐπί κατοχῆς ἐθνικόν ἀγῶνα* [Ella Turk, Inc. Recognition of a Contribution to the National Struggle during the Occupation] (Athens, 1945). Both books deal largely with the contribution of "Ella Turk" to the Greek supply problem.

Bakopoulos, Constantinos Th. *'Η ὁμηρία τῶν 5 ἀντιστρατήγων* [The Internment of the 5 Lieutenant-Generals] (Athens, 1948). /1,5,R/ Intentions and activities of the Papagos group ("Military Hierarchy") and their subsequent internment in various German concentration camps.

Bamboures, Epam. *Τό 'Ελληνικόν ἐμπορικόν ναυτικόν κατά τόν τελευταῖον πόλεμον* [The Greek Merchant Navy in the Recent War] (Athens, 1949).

Barker, Dudley. *Grivas. Portrait of a Terrorist* (London, 1959). /7/

Barker, Elisabeth. *Macedonia. Its Place in Balkan Power Politics* (London/New York, 1950). /7/

Bartolini, Alfonso. *Storia della Resistenza Italiana all'Estero* (Padova, 1965). /1,2,3,6,7,8,L/ Much information particularly about the events after the Italian capitulation (Acqui, Pinerolo Divisions).

Bartziotas, Vasiles G. *'Εθνική 'Αντίσταση καί Δεκέμβρης 1944* [National Resistance and the December 1944] (Athens: Synchrone Epoche, 1979)./1,2,6,7,L/ The author was secretary of the KOA (Communist Party Organization of Athens) during the occupation. His "orthodox" analysis of KKE policy and of pertinent post-war historiography is prominent in both aspects by censuring nearly everyone. However, the passages containing his own reminiscences repeatedly provide yet unknown information—even if they should be read with some caution.

Beikos, Georgoulas, *EAM καί Λαϊκή Αὐτοδιοίκηση. Μιά προσωπική μαρτυρία γιά τό θεσμό ὅπως ἐφαρμόστηκε στήν ἐλεύθερη Εὐρυτανία* [EAM and People's Self-Government. A Personal Testimony on the Institution as it was Applied in Free Evrytania] (Thessaloniki, 1976). /1,2,6,L/

———. *Λαϊκή ἐξουσία στήν ἐλεύθερη 'Ελλάδα* [People's Rule in Free Greece] 2 Vols. (Athens: Themelio, 1979).

———. "'Η κατοχική λαϊκή αὐτοδιοίκηση καί δικαιοσύνη" [People's Self-Government and Justice During the Occupation], *Anti,* 16.8.75, 14–16.

Bekios-Lambros, Spyros. *Σελίδες ἀπό τήν 'Εθνική 'Αντίσταση* [Pages from the National Resistance] (Athens: Velouchi, 1976). /2,5,L/.

Belčev, T. "Pečatot i najaktnelnite problemi vo nego za vreme na okupacijata (1941–1945) i ponea vo Egejska Makedonija" [The Press in Aegean Macedonia and the Most Vital Problems of This Country during the Occupation Years 1941–1945], *Glasnik na Institutot za nationalna Istorija,* Skopje, XVI: 1 (1972), 135–164. Not consulted.

Benorogia, Avraam. "Στά χέρια τῶν Χιτλερικῶν" [In the Hands of the Hitlerites], *Anti,* 26.5.79, 32–34./5,L/. Reminiscences by the Jewish founder of the "Federación."

Benetatos, Dionysios. *Σημειώσεις ἀπό τήν ἱστορία τῆς ἐθνικῆς διαίρεσης* [Notes from the History of the National Division] (Athens, 1947).

———. *Τό χρονικό τῆς κατοχῆς 1941–1944* [The Chronicle of the Occupation 1941–1944] (Athens, 1963). /1,2,6,8/ This amended and enlarged version of the above-mentioned work provides many unknown details on the genesis of EAM, the subsequent withdrawal of some moderate socialist groups and their desperate attempts to steer a middle course between the extreme Left and the royalist Right. A largely objective and sensible account which sometimes exaggerates the activities and the significance of the organizations led by the author.

———. *'Η ἕνωση τῆς Εὐρώπης καί τό 'Ελληνικό πρόβλημα* [The Union of Europe and the Greek Problem] (Athens, 1974). /1,2,6,7/ A collection of articles, some of them containing summaries or supplementary material on the problems of the occupation and the resistance.

Benyon-Tinker, W.E. *Dust Upon the Sea* (London, 1947)./5/ Reminiscences on commando raids in the Eastern Aegean.

Berates, Yiannes. *'Οδοιπορικό τοῦ 43* [Itinerary of 1943] (Athens, 1946). /2,5/ An EDES andarte (the author), gradually disillusioned with the guerrilla movement, leaves again for Athens.

Birkas, Costas. *Γιατί πολεμήσαμε—'Η ἀλήθεια καί τό ψεῦδος γιά τήν 'Εθνική 'Αντίσταση* [Why We Fought—Truth and Lie Regarding the National Resistance] (Athens, 1956). 2nd ed.: (Athens: Kastaniotes, 1975). /1,2,L/.

———. *'Η ἐποποιΐα τῆς 'Εθνικῆς 'Αντίστασης 1941–1944* [The Epic of the National Resistance 1941–1944] (Athens, 1960). /1,2,L/. This enlarged version is a very lengthy dithyramb (and simultaneously an apology) for EAM/ELAS.

Bobotinos, Y. *Συμμαχικαί ἀποστολαί ἐν 'Ελλάδι 1941–1945* (Allied Missions in Greece 1941–1945) (Athens, 1952). /1,6,R/ The author was leader of a minor right-wing organization.

Borkenau, Franz. *Der europäische Kommunismus* (Munich, 1953). /1,2,7/ The author deals with Greece on pp. 383–410. His thesis that KKE (and EAM) followed Moscow's dictates down to the smallest details is indefensible and reveals—as does the entire work—the strong anticommunist feelings of a former communist.

Bosnakides, S. *Οἱ μικροί ἥρωες τῆς ἐθνικῆς ἀντίστασης 1940–1944* [The Small Heroes of the National Resistance, 1940–1944]. 2nd ed.: (Athens: by the author, 1976). /2,6,L/ Describes the important contribution of some children to the intelligence network of EAM/ELAS.

Bouloukos, Aristos. "'Η 'Εθνική 'Αντίστασις στήν Πελοπόννησο" [The National Resistance in the Peloponnesus], *Ethnikos Keryx*, 26.2.61-21.4.63. /1,2,6,R/

Bourdaras, Alkiviades N. Letter in *To Vema*, 24.6.48. /4,5/ The author claims the "parentage" of the "Sacred Battalion" for himself. Only partially justified.

Bragadin, Marc'Antonio. *The Italian Navy in World War II* (Annapolis, Md.: U.S. Naval Institute, 1957).

Bramos, Costas. *Σλαβοκομμουνιστικαί ὀργανώσεις ἐν Μακεδονία: Προπαγάνδα καί ἐπαναστατική δρᾶσις* [Slav-Communist Organizations in Macedonia: Propaganda and Revolutionary Activities] (Thessaloniki, 1953). /R/ The work is severely marred by an unfortunate mixing of authentic and faked material designed to negate the "national reliability" of KKE.

Brandt, Karl, Schiller, Otto, and Ahlgrimm, Franz. *Management of Agriculture and Food in the German-Occupied and Other Areas of Fortress Europe* (Stanford, 1953). /3,7/ Contains good review article on Greece (pp. 233–248).

Brillakes, Antones. "ΕΠΟΝ Κρήτης" [EPON of Crete], *Anti*, No. 13, 22.2.75, pp. 28–30./1,6.L/.

Brockdorf, Werner. *Geheimkommandos des Zweiten Weltkrieges* (Munich, 1968). /3,7/

Bruns, Diedrich. *Grenadier-Regiment 16 (1939–1945)* (Wiesbaden, 1959). /2,3,5,7/ A regiment commander gives his impressions from the last occupation phase of Crete and the German withdrawal from Greece.

Buckley, Christopher. *Five Ventures* (London: HMSO, 1954). Contains a fairly good review of the struggle for the Dodecanese (autumn 1943).

Bürker, Ulrich. "Einsatz in Griechenland." In *Furchtlos und Treu* (Cologne, 1971), 59–70. /2,3,5/ German staff officer gives his war impressions of occupied Epirus and of the area commander, General Lanz.

Burks, R.V. "Statistical Profile of the Greek Communist." *Journal of Modern History*, XXVII (1955), 153–158.

———. *The Dynamics of Communism in Eastern Europe* (Princeton, N.J.: Princeton University Press, 1961). Despite its highly questionable methods and conclusions, this remains a widely quoted and interesting work.

Byford-Jones, W. *The Greek Trilogy. (Resistance—Liberation—Revolution).* (London, 1945). /1,6,7/ Author entered Greece as a press officer immediately after the liberation. Concerning the occupation period, his interesting report relies therefore on hearsay evidence—with all its faults.

Canouta-Capsambelis, Pothoula. *From a Balcony in Athens, 1940–1944* (Alexandria, n.d.=1946). /1,5/

Capell, Richard. *Simiomata, a Greek Note Book 1944–45* (London, 1946). /1,2,6,7/ A well-written but biased account. The author, correspondent of the *Daily Telegraph*, applauds official British policy and criticizes EAM vehemently. This attitude springs mainly from interviews with BLOs.

Carey, Jane P.C. and Carey, Andrew G. *The Web of Modern Greek Politics* (New York and London: Columbia University Press, 1968). The authors briefly review the years 1941–44 (pp. 124–148).

Caroff, M. "La Marine Italienne pendant la Guerre." *Revue d'Histoire de la Deuxième Guerre Mondiale*, XXXIX (July 1960), 15–22. /7/

Cavalli, D. Giuseppe. *Il calvario di due ammiragli. Ricordi d'un compagno di carcere*. 2nd ed. (Parma, 1955). /5,7/ Source deals with the Italian commanders of Cos and Rhodes, executed by the Mussolini regime in 1944 because of their cooperation with Allied forces in September 1943.

Chalkias, Nikos S. "'Η κατά τῆς Βολισσοῦ ἐξόρμησις τῶν Γερμανῶν τό καλοκαίρι τοῦ 1944" [The German Attack against Volissos in the Summer of 1944], *Chiake Epitheorese*, XI: 31 (Feb. 1973), 66–68. Deals with the last phase of the occupation in Chios.

Chandler, Geoffrey. *The Divided Land: An Anglo-Greek Tragedy* (London and New York, 1959). /2,5,7/ Good source for the transition period at the end of the occupation. (Author entered Greece in September 1944.)

Charokopos, Georgios E. *Τό φρούριον Κρήτης. 'Ο μυστικός πόλεμος 1941–1944* [Fortress Crete. The Secret War 1941–1944] (Athens, 1971). /1,2,6,R/

———. *'Η ἀπαγωγή τοῦ στρατηγοῦ Κράϊπε* [The Kidnapping of General Kreipe] (Athens: Ide, 1973). /2,3,6/

Chatzeanastasiou, A. "'Η ὀργάνωσις *'X'* " [The Organization "X"], *Ethnikos Keryx*, 10.12.55-31.3.56. /1,6,R/

Chatzepanagiotou, Yiannes G. (Thomas). *'Η πολιτική διαθήκη τοῦ Ἄρη Βελουχιώτη* [The Political Testament of Ares Velouchiotes] (Athens: Dorikos, 1975). / 2,6,L/ This work, introduced and edited by Ares' brother (Babes Klaras), contains much useful, even if somewhat panegyrical, information about ELAS and its "archikapetanios" Ares—as long as the author relies on personal experience. His wider conclusions and theories are often contestable or erroneous (e.g., those concerning the allegedly suspect or even "treacherous" role of the communist leader Siantos).

Chatzephotes, I. M. "Τά *Δωδεκάνησα 'Ελεύθερα*" [The Dodecanesus Is Free], *Historia*, 59 (May 1973), 22–29.

Chatzes, Thanases. *'Η νικηφόρα ἐπανάσταση πού χάθηκε (1941–1945)* [The Victorious Revolution Which Was Lost, 1941–1945]. 2 Vols. (Athens: Papazeses, 1977–1978). /1,2,6,8,L/ The communist secretary-general of EAM provides extremely valuable information, particularly concerning the inner-party discussion of strategy as well as the relationship between the KKE and the non-communist EAM. This often pungent account is based on the author's notebooks and the archives of the KKE. However, beyond his own sphere, Chatzes is repeatedly mistaken.

Chatzopoulos, Achileas. *Οἱ προστάτες 1943–1949* [The Protectors 1943–1949] (Athens: Papazeses, 1977). /1,7/ Contains only a short summary on the occupation period.

Choutas, Stylianos Th. *'Η 'Εθνική 'Αντίστασις τῶν 'Ελλήνων* [The National Resistance of the Greeks] (Athens, 1961). /2,6/ Author was EDES chieftain for the Valtos region. He provides personal recollections and many informative documents from the EDES archives, but belittles systematically the resistance record of ELAS.

Christie-Miller, W. "Peloponnesus, 1944." *Quis separabit* XVII: 1 (1950), 62–67. An account by the British officer who escorted Kanellopoulos to the Peloponnesus on the eve of liberation. Special emphasis is given to relations with ELAS and the negotiations with the Security Battalions.

Christopoulos, Andreas Ch. (Phoivos) *Οἱ Ἰταλογερμανοί στήν Ἀργολίδα* [The Italians and Germans in Argolis] (Nauplia, 1946). /1,2,3,6/ Consists of numerous 'vignettes' offering a vivid, and often first-hand, account of everyday life under the occupation, as well as descriptions of outstanding events.

Chrysochoou, Athan. I. *Ἡ κατοχή ἐν Μακεδονίᾳ* [The Occupation in Macedonia]. 6 vols. (Thessaloniki, 1949–52). /1,3,6,R/ This violently anti-communist source (by a prominent collaborator) should be used with considerable caution.

Churchill, Winston S. *The Second World War* (London, 1950–53). References to Greece are to be found especially in vols. V and VI.

Clogg, Richard. " 'Pearls from Swine': The Foreign Office Papers, SOE and the Greek Resistance." In Phyllis Auty and Richard Clogg (eds.), *British Policy towards Wartime Resistance in Yugoslavia and Greece* (London: Macmillan, 1975), 167–205. A discerning study giving due weight to the decisive visit by a resistance delegation to Cairo in summer 1943.

Collotti, Enzo. "La resistenza Greca tra storia e politica." *Il Movimento di Liberazione in Italia*, 88 (1967), 47–56.

Condit, D.M. *Case Study in Guerrilla War: Greece during World War II* (Washington, D.C., 1961). Balanced and detailed study prepared at the American University by the Special Operations Research Office under contract with the U.S. Department of the Army.

Czech, Danuta. "Deportation und Vernichtung der griechischen Juden im KL Auschwitz." *Hefte von Auschwitz*, 11 (1970), 5–37. English, French, and Russian summaries: pp. 201,204,207.

Dalianis, Costas. "Der nationale antifaschistische Widerstandskampf des griechischen Volkes 1941–1944." Unpublished Ph.D. Dissertation, Leipzig University, 1970./L/ Lacks any evidence based on primary sources and is based on virtually a few memoirs; some of the most important are mentioned as "not consulted, because not available in the GDR." The author attempts to fill the pages by frequent quotations from Marxist "classics."

Daphnes, Gregorios. *Σοφοκλῆς Ἐλευθερίου Βενιζέλος, 1894–1964* [Sophocles Eleftheriou Venizelos, 1894–1964] (Athens: Ikaros, 1970). /4,7/ Biography commissioned by the Venizelos family.

Daphnes, Constantinos. *Χρόνια πολέμου καί κατοχῆς. Κέρκυρα 1940–1944* [Years of War and Occupation. Corfu 1940–1944] (Corfu: Kerkyraika Chronika, 1966). /1,3,6/

Daravales, Noules. *Ἡ χρυσή λίρα ἀπό Ἀπριλίου 1941 μέχρι καί σήμερον* [The Gold Sovereign from April 1941 to the Present] (Athens, 1946).

Deakin, F.W. "Great Britain and European Resistance," In *European Resistance Movements, Second Conference* (*infra*), 98–119, 643–646.

Dedouses, Ioannes D. *Θύμιος Δεδούσης, λοχαγός—βουλευτής, ὁ ἐθνομάρτυς ἀγωνιστής* [Thymios Dedousis, Captain—Deputy, the Martyred Fighter]

(Athens, 1949). /2,5,R/ Fanatically anti-communist account of the 5/42 Regiment of EKKA and its royalist extreme wing, Dedouses. Written by his brother and companion.

Delivanis, Demetrios and Cleveland, William C. *Greek Monetary Developments 1939–1948. A Case Study of the Consequences of World War II for the Monetary System of a Small Nation* (Bloomington, Indiana, 1949).

Demetriades, Demetres N. *Φλόγες ἀπό τήν ἀντάρτικη ἐποποιΐα* [Flames from the Guerrilla Epic]. 2nd ed. (Athens, 1965). /2,5,L/

Demetriades, Giorgos V. *Περπατῶντας στ' ἀγκαθοτόπια.* [Walking on Thorny Ground] (Athens: by the author, 1978). /2,6,L/ Reminiscences and information on the activities of the Epirote ELAS, with particular emphasis on the alleged murder of the leftist (Greek-born) BLO "Lawrence" by the BMM leadership.

Demetriou, A.K. *'Η πρώτη ἀπεργία στήν σκλαβωμένη Εὐρώπη. Χρονικό τῆς κατοχῆς* [The First Strike in Enslaved Europe. Chronicle of the Occupation] (Athens, 1945). /1,6/

Demetriou, Dem. N. (Nikephoros). *'Αντάρτης στά βουνά τῆς Ρούμελης. Χρονικό 1940–44* [Guerrilla in the Mountains of Roumeli. Chronicle 1940–44]. 3 vols. (Athens, 1965). /2,5,L/ Author was the first ELAS officer in the mountains. His interesting, but often apologetic account deals almost equally with the ELAS conflicts with the occupation forces and with Psarros' rival guerrilla organization (5/42 Regiment).

———. *'Ελληνική ἐμπειρία 1944–67* [Greek Experience 1944–67] (Athens, 1971). A pungent criticism of more than twenty years of leftist politics.

Demetriou, D. *Τά φοβερά ντοκουμέντα. Γοργοπόταμος: Ἕλληνες ἀντάρτες ἐναντίον τοῦ Ρόμμελ.* [The Horrible Documents. Gorgopotamos: Greek Guerrillas against Rommel] (Athens: Typos, 1975).

Demotakes, Nikolaos. *Μυστικός πόλεμος 1941–1944: Μίδας/Πλούτων* [Secret War 1941–1944: Midas/Plouton] (Athens, 1948). /1,6/ The author was leading member of these two very significant espionage and sabotage organizations.

Depos, Eleftherios. "'Η διάσπασις ἀρχίζει εἰς τόν ΕΔΕΣ 'Αθηνῶν (*'Οκτώβριος 1942–Μάϊος 1943*)" [The Split Begins in the EDES of Athens (October 1942–May 1943)]. *Historikon Archeion Ethnikes Antistaseos*, Nos. 7–8, 22–24, 27–28, through 41–43 (1958–1962). /1,3,5/ The author was secretary of the non-collaborating EDES faction in Athens and describes his sad experiences during the progressive disintegration of EDES.

Dertiles, Panagiotes V. *'Αριθμοί καί κείμενα τῶν ἐξόδων κατοχῆς καί ἡ ἀξίωσις τῆς 'Ελλάδος* [Data and Documents concerning the Occupation Costs and the Greek Claim] (Athens, 1964).

Despotopoulos, K. "Ποιός ἔδωκεν εἰς τούς Ἄγγλους τό δικαίωμα τῆς ἐπεμβάσεως;" [Who Gave the English the Right to Intervene?], *To Vema*, 24.10,64. /2,5,L/ The EAM delegate at the Caserta Conference argues that the (amended) treaty cannot be quoted as legal justification for the British intervention in December 1944.

Diakow, J. *Generaloberst Alexander Löhr.* (Freiburg, 1964). /3,7 / Biography of the German High Commander in Greece, executed in 1947.

Diamantopoulos, Iakovos. *Ὦ Εἰρήνη! Ὀδοιπορικό 40–44* [O, Peace! Itinerary 1940–44] (Athens: Hellenikos Ekdotikos Organismos, 1974). /1,5,R/ Resistance practised in the hospital sphere.

Dionysios, Metropolitan of Lemnos *Πιστοί ἄχρι θανάτου* [Faithful until Death] (Athens, 1959). /7,R/

Dixon, Piers. *Double Diploma* (London, 1968). /5,7 / Author was a Foreign Office official and Eden's private secretary. Scattered throughout are some useful references to Greece, e.g., Papandreou's talks with Churchill in Rome (Aug. 1944).

Djoumalieff, Stancho. *The Greco-Bulgarian Frontier, the Aegean and Greek Territorial Claims* (Sofia, 1946).

Doumas, Demetrios I. *'Ιστορικαί ἀναμνήσεις καί αὐτοβιογραφία* [Historical Reminiscences and Autobiography]. 2nd ed. (Ioannina, 1969). /1,2,3,5,7/ Informative source about the occupation of Epirus and especially Ioannina. Author took part in the delegation which negotiated on behalf of the German authorities with the Epirot resistance leaders (Oct. 1943).

Doxiades, Constantine A. *Θυσίες τῆς Ἑλλάδος, αἰτήματα καί ἐπανορθώσεις στόν Β΄ Παγκόσμιο Πόλεμο* [Sacrifices of Greece, Claims and Reparations in the Second World War] (Athens, 1947).

———. *Such was the War in Greece* (Athens, 1947). Two of Doxiades' numerous relevant publications (with much statistical data), issued in his capacity as Under-Secretary of Reconstruction in 1946–47.

Drakos, Th. "Ἕλληνες σωτῆρες Ἄγγλων στήν κατοχή: *Μέ τόν σταυρό καί τό τσεκούρι.*" [Greek Saviors of Englishmen during the Occupation: With Crucifix and Axe], *Akropolis* 30.6.–29.7.55.

Dzelepy, E.N. *Le drame de la résistance Grecque* (Paris, 1946). /1,2,4,L/

EAM, Central Committee. *Δήμιοι καί θύματα* [Executioners and Victims] (Athens, 1945). /1,3,7,L/ Occasionally exaggerated reports on atrocities during the occupation and its aftermath, committed by Germans, British, and their respective Greek collaborators.

EAM, 6th sector. *Ἀνατολικές συνοικίες Ἀθήνας 1941–1945* [The Eastern Neighborhoods of Athens, 1941–1945] (Athens, 1945). /1,6,L/

Eden, Anthony (The Earl of Avon). *The Eden Memoirs: The Reckoning.* vol. III. (London), 1965). /5,7 /

Ehrenstrale, Hans. *Fredsmäklare i Grekland. Med Röd Korset bland partisaner, patrioter, Patrasiter* (Stockholm, 1945). The International Red Cross delegate in Patras recalls his successful negotiations with EAM/ELAS, British commandos, German authorities, and collaborating Security Battalions.

Ehrman, John. *Grand Strategy,* ed. J.R.M. Butler (London: HMSO, 1956). /7/ Author presents the official British position on World War II.

Eirenaios (Metropolitan). *'Η δύναμις τοῦ 'Ελληνοχριστιανικοῦ πνεύματος. Ἀναμνήσεις καί ἐντυπώσεις ἀπό τήν κατοχήν τῆς νήσου Σάμου καί τήν Μέσην Ἀνατολήν* [The Power of the Greek Christian Spirit. Reminiscences and Impressions from the Occupation of Samos and from the Middle East] (Athens, 1948). /1,2,3,4,5/ Especially interesting are the chapters dealing with the attempts to establish a defensible united front consisting of Italian troops, British commandos, and the whole spectrum of Greek forces, following Italy's change of sides.

Elephantes, Angelos. "EAM: ἱστορία καί ἰδεολογία. Προϋποθέσεις γιά μιά ἐπιστημονική θεώρηση τοῦ EAM" [EAM: History and Ideology. Preconditions for a Scholarly Estimation of EAM] *Polites* 3/4 (August 1976), 63–68. /L/

Eliou, Philippos, ed. "'Η συνάντησή μας μέ τόν Στάλιν. 'Αναμνήσεις τοῦ Μήτσου Παρτσαλίδη καταγραμμένες ἀπό τόν Φίλιππο 'Ηλιοῦ" [Our Meeting with Stalin. Metsos Partsalides' recollections Recorded by Philippos Eliou] *Avge* 29.2.–3.3.76. /7/

Enciclopedia dell' antifascismo e della resistenza (Milano: La Pietra, 1971). Various entries deal with the occupation of Greece. See especially: A. Ba. (= Alfonso Bartolini), "Grecia," in vol. II, 647–657.

Enepekides, Polychrones C. *'Η 'Ελληνική 'Αντίστασις 1941–1944* [The Greek Resistance 1941–1944] (Athens: Hestia, 1964). A number of Wehrmacht records (unfortunately not identified by their fascicle number), connected by some vague remarks by the author. The appendix contains the interesting, even if often polemical, comments of some protagonists of the resistance.

———. "'Η *'Τελική Λύσις' εἰς τήν 'Ελλάδα διά πρώτην φοράν εἰς φῶς*" [The "Final Solution" in Greece Brought to Light for the First Time], *To Vema*, 21.8.–13.9.66. Book edition: *Οἱ διωγμοί τῶν 'Εβραίων ἐν 'Ελλάδι, 1941–1944* [The persecution of the Jews in Greece, 1941–1944] (Athens, Papazeses, 1969). Study on the extermination of Greek Jewry based largely on German records.

"'Επέτηχε ἤ ἀπέτηχε τό EAM;" [Did the EAM Succeed or Fail?], *Kathemerine*, 25.–28.9.76. The proceedings of a discussion held at the BBC with contributions by Apostolou, Chatzes, Despotopoulos, Hammond, Myers, Stringos, and Woodhouse.

Ephraimides, Vasiles. "Τό πολιτικό σύστημα κατοχῆς τῶν Χιτλεροφασιστων στήν 'Ελλάδα" [The Political Occupation System of the Hitlero-Fascists in Greece], *Ethnike Antistase*, 7 (August 1964), 684–694. /L/

Epirus. Four Years of Resistance. (Sacrifices and Holocausts). Published by the Prefecture of Arta. (Athens, 1945).

Ethnike Allelengye. *Μία προσπάθεια κι ἕνας ἄθλος. Τό ἔργο τῆς 'Εθνικῆς 'Αλληλεγγύης 'Ελλάδος* [Endeavor and Achievement. The Work of the National Solidarity of Greece] (Athens, 1945). /1,L/

———. *Τέσσερα χρόνια ἀγῶνες καί δράση τῆς ΕΑ Θεσσαλονίκης* [Four Years of Struggle and Action of the Thessaloniki EA] (Thessaloniki, 1945). Two accounts by the EA, the "Red Cross of EAM," which cared not only for EAM members.

Eudes, Dominique. *Les Kapetanios. La guerre civile grecque de 1943 à 1949* (Paris: Fayard, 1970). English edition (London, 1972); Greek edition (Athens: Exantas, 1975). The main hypothesis of this well-written and interesting, but somewhat melodramatic work overlooks the real reasons for the tension between some chieftains of ELAS (particularly Ares) and the party establishment. Instead, the author posits a fundamental rift between the "Titoist kapetanios," striving for a peasant-based guerrilla warfare and for a subsequent agrarian revolution, and on the other hand the "ossified" dogmatists, possessed by the "atavistic

Stalinist suspicion of the peasantry" and generally of partisan warfare, and favoring the traditional patterns of urban "proletarian struggle" (demonstrations, strikes, etc.). As it is known, similar tendencies existed during the civil war (1946–49), which is not the subject of this bibliography. So Eudes' position is largely correct as to the second part of his book. But he is wrong when he extrapolates to the occupation period (except its early phase, when the mentioned "Stalinist" doubts on the practicability of "andartiko" were fully justified)—and is certainly incorrect about events in 1943, the year he begins with. According to Eudes, nearly all woe in recent Greek history should be traced back to the unfortunate triumph of the Stalinist view in 1943–44. Apart from some other errors and confusions the author does not seem to know the original "Titoist" view about the "unreliability" of the peasant class. Remarkably, it was Stalin himself who urged the Yugoslav comrades to discontinue their visible preference for "proletarian units."

European Resistance Movements 1939–45. First International Conference, held at Lièges—Bruxelles—Berendonk 1958 (Oxford, 1960).

European Resistance Movements 1939–45. Second International Conference, held at Milan 1961 (Oxford, 1964).

Ewerth, Lutz. "Der Arbeitseinsatz von Landesbewohnern besetzter Gebiete des Ostens und Südostens im Zweiten Weltkrieg." Unpublished LL.D. Dissertation, Tübingen University, 1954. Provides many data on the voluntary engagement of Greek workers in Germany during 1941–44 and their considerable "lack of diligence."

Fielding, Xan. *Hide and Seek. The Story of a War-time Agent* (London: Secker and Warburg, 1954). Candid account by a BLO to the Cretan resistance.

Fino, Edoardo. *La tragedia di Rodi e dell' Egeo* (Rome, 1957). /3,6/ Events before and after the Italian capitulation.

Fleischer, Hagen. "Πῶς ἔβλεπε τό ΚΚΕ τήν ἀντίσταση" [How the KKE Saw the Resistance], *Anti*, No. 18, 3.5.75, pp. 11–16. Study of sources, attempting to disclose the original conception of the communist leadership as to the preferable pattern of resistance (and especially concerning guerrilla warfare).

———. "The 'Anomalies' in the Greek Middle East Forces, 1941–1944," *Journal of the Hellenic Diaspora*, V:3 (1978), 5–36. /4/ Based on the pertinent chapters of a forthcoming comprehensive 'political history' of occupation and resistance in Greece.

Fleming, D.F. *The Cold War and Its Origins*. Vol. I. (New York, 1961). /7/

Formato, Romualdo. *L'eccidio di Cefalonia*. (Rome, 1946). /3/ Greek translation: *Ethnikos Keryx*, 16.11.47–17.1.48. Deals with the resistance of the Acqui Division after the Italian capitulation and the bloody German reprisals (Sept. 1943).

Forster, Edward S. *A Short History of Modern Greece* (New York, 1956). /7/

Franco, Hizkia M. *Les Martyrs Juifs de Rhodes et de Cos* (Elizabethville, 1952).

Franz, Hermann. *Gebirgsjäger der Polizei. 1942–1945* (Bad Nauheim: Podzun, 1963). /2,3,6,7/ The author was for more than a year commander of the police forces (not the SS) stationed in Greece. Much useful—though biased—information about ELAS operations and German retaliation.

Freeman, John et al., eds. *Ξενοκρατία—Τό ἀποκαλυπτικό χρονικό τῶν ξένων ἐπεμβάσεων στήν 'Ελλάδα (1944–1974)* [Foreign Rule—The Revealing Chronicle of Foreign Interventions in Greece (1944–1974)] (Athens: Papyros, 1975). /7/

Fricke, Gert. "Das Unternehmen des XXII. Gebirgsarmeekorps gegen die Inseln Kefalonia und Korfu im Rahmen des Falles "Achse" (September 1943)." *Militärgeschichtliche Mitteilungen,* I: 1 (1967), 31–58. Same subject as Formato (*supra*), based on German records.

Friederike, Königin der Hellenen. *Erfahrungen* (Tübingen, 1971). English edition: Frederica. *A Measure of Understanding* (London, 1971); Greek edition: (Athens, 1971). /4,5,7,R/. Memoirs containing a mixture of useful, useless, and questionable information about the then Crown-Princess's years in South Africa and the Middle East.

Gaitanides, Johannes. *Greichenland ohne Säulen* (Munich, 1955). /7,R/

Gardner, Hugh H. *Guerrilla and Counterguerrilla Warfare in Greece, 1941–1945* (Washington, D.C., 1962). /2,3 / This study, which is based on German records, is difficult to find in Europe. Not consulted.

Gatopoulos, D. *'Ιστορία τῆς κατοχῆς* [History of the Occupation]. 4 vols. (Athens, 1949). New edition: (Athens: Melissa, n.d.). /1,3,6 / In spite of its errors and gaps (particularly regarding guerrilla warfare) still one of the most detailed and impartial publications. Annex contains numerous political anecdotes, recreating superbly the spirit of the period.

Geladopoulos, Philippas. *13η Μεραρχία τοῦ ΕΛΑΣ* [The 13th Division of ELAS] (Athens, 1975). /1,2,5,L/

Georgiou, V. "Τό ἱστορικό ἔργο τῆς ΠΕΕΑ" [The Historic Work of PEEA], *Kommounistike Epitheorese,* 31–32 (Oct.–Nov. 1944), 15–17.

Georgiou, Vasos et al., eds. *1940–1945. 'Ιστορία τῆς ἀντίστασης* [1940–1945. History of the Resistance]. 6 vols. (Athens: Avlos, 1979). /7/ This copious and profusely illustrated deluxe edition contains nearly all information that could be derived from the bulk of (mainly) pro-EAM publications. Lacks any really new material.

Ghilardini, Luigi. *I martiri di Cefalonia* (Milan, 1952). Same subject as Formato (*supra*).

Giannaros, Gregorios. "Γιατί '*Διπλή 'Αποκατάσταση*';" [Why "Double Vindication"?], *Kommounistike Theoria kai Politike,* 25 (Oct.–Nov. 1978), 78–86. Interview with M. Partsalides on his book of the same name (*infra*).

Gitlin, Todd. "Counter-Insurgency: Myth and Reality in Greece." In D. Horowitz, ed., *Containment and Revolution* (London, 1967), 140–181. /1,2,7,L/

Gotzamanes, Soterios. *Κατοχικόν δάνειον καί δαπάναι κατοχῆς* [Occupation Loan and Occupation Costs] (Thessaloniki, 1954).

Gotzes, Ioannes. *Φλόγες στόν Ὄλυμπο* [Flames on Olympus] (Athens, 1945). /1,2,3,5/

Gonatas, Stylianos E. *'Απομνημονεύματα 1897–1957* [Memoirs 1897–1957] (Athens, 1958). Understandably, the author hardly deals with his own activities during the occupation years.

Görlitz, Walter. *Der Zweite Weltkrieg 1939–1945.* 2 vols. (Stuttgart, 1951). /2,3,7/

G.P.K. "Συμβολή στή μελέτη τῆς 'Αντίστασης" [Contribution to the

Study of the Resistance], *Dialogos*, 9–10 (April 1974). /1,2,L/

Grammatikakes, Yiannes (Astrapogiannes). *Πῶς πολεμήσαμε* [How We Fought] (Sparta, 1945). /1,2,L/ Memorandum on the resistance merits of the Peloponnesian ELAS, defending the execution of a "total of 228 collaborators."

Grassmann, Gerhard O. *Die deutsche Besatzungsgesetzgebung während des Zweiten Weltkrieges* (Tübingen, 1958). /3,7/

Greece. Bureau Hellenique d'Information. *La Calvaire de la Grèce. Quatre années de lutte, de souffrances et de gloire* (Paris, n.d.[=1945?]).

Gregoriades, Phoivos, N. *Τό ἀντάρτικο* [The Guerrilla Movement]. 5 vols. (Athens: Kamarinopoulos, 1964). /1,2,6,8 / The author, one of the first officers to join ELAS and a post-war journalist of right-wing newspapers, has collected (and published at intervals) much material concerning the guerrilla movement. This voluminous compilation represents as yet the best (i.e., the least partial) source for the "andartiko," as it tries to do justice also to ELAS's rival organizations EDES and EKKA. Less dependable for events outside the guerrilla sphere.

Gregoriades, Solon N. *'Ιστορία τῆς Συγχρόνου 'Ελλάδος 1941–1967* [History of Contemporary Greece 1941–1967]. vols.I, II. (Athens: Kapopoulos, 1973). /1,2,3,4/ The author is brother of Ph. G. (see above) and likewise former ELAS officer. Concerning his broader subject, the balanced narrative contains fewer errors (and less sophisticated "analysis") than most other circulating "Histories." One of the best attempts to survey the entire period of the occupation.

Gregoriou, Emmanouel Th. *Τό βουλγαρικόν ὄργιον αἵματος εἰς τήν Δυτικήν Μακεδονίαν (1941–1944)* [The Bulgarian Blood Orgy in Western Macedonia (1941–1944)] (Athens, 1947). /1,3,6,R/

Grivas, Georgios. *The Memoirs of General Grivas*. ed. C. Foley (New York and Washington, 1965). /1,5,7,R/ As prolegomena to the history of EOKA, the memoirs extol Grivas' extreme right-wing organization "X".

Grivas, Kleanthes. *'Ελλάδα 1940–1974. Προσπάθεια ἑρμηνείας τῶν πολιτικῶν ἐξελίξεων στή χώρα μας* [Greece 1940–1974. An Attempt at an Interpretation of the Political Developments in Our Country] (Athens: Dialogos, 1974).

Gubbins, Sir Colin. "Resistance Movements in the War." *Journal of the Royal United Service Institution*, 93 (1948), 210–223. /1,2,6,7/ Useful background material about SOE by its former director.

Günther-Hornig, Margot. *Kunstschutz in den von Deutschland besetzten Gebieten 1939–1945* (Tübingen, 1958). /3,7 / One chapter (pp. 63–78) deals with the protection of Greek art treasures and of archaeological discoveries by the German authorities.

Gyiokas, Panagiotes. "Οἱ Σβῶλος—Τσιριμῶκος ἐπαγιδεύθησαν ἀπό τό KKE" [Svolos and Tsirimokos were Trapped by the KKE], *Akropolis*, 8.–10.3.73. The author was a leading member of Tsirimokos' ELD until December 1944.

Hahn, Paul. *Die griechische Währung und währungspolitische Massnahmen unter der Besetzung 1941–1944* (Tübingen, 1957). /3,6,8/

Hall, D.O.W. *Escapes* (Wellington: Department of Internal Affairs, War Histories Branch, 1954). /5/ Deals with the escapes of New Zealanders prisoners of war, with the support of the Greek population.

Hampe, Roland. "Besprechung des griechischen und zweier englischer Kunstschutzberichte (Kriegsschäden an Altertümern)" *Gnomon*, 22 (1950), 1–17. /3,6/

———. *Die Rettung Athens im Oktober 1944* (Wiesbaden: Steiner, 1955). /3,5/ Valuable account by a representative of German counterespionage ("Ic") concerning his negotiations for the declaration of Athens as "open city" in return for an unmolested German retreat from Attica. A Greek translation was published in *Athenaike* (16.5.–1.6.55), and a considerably abridged version in *Ta Nea* (20.–30.5.55), followed by comments by some protagonists (Dakos, Zalokostas, Tsironikos, and others).

Hamrin, Agne. *Grekland mellan Öst och Väst* (Stockholm, 1948). /7/

Hamson, Denys. *We Fell Among Greeks.* 2nd ed. (London, 1947). /2,5,7 / Author was a member of the famous British commando "Harling," which was parachuted into Greece in order to interrupt the important north-south railway (Gorgopotamos). Soon after this success, Hamson clearly became fed up with his involuntary, continued stay as BLO, with guerrillas "of all colours," and even with some of his BLO colleagues. Nevertheless, an exciting account.

"'Η ἀγωνία καί τό μαρτύριο ἑνός λαοῦ (6 *'Απριλίου* 1941-*'Οκτώβριος* 1944)" [The Agony and the Martyrdom of a People (6 April 1941–October 1944)], *Ethnikos Keryx*, 28.3.48–1949. /1,3,R/

"'Η ἀλήθεια γιά τήν 'Εθνική 'Αντίσταση" [The Truth about the National Resistance], *Rizospastis*, 23.9.79 ff.

"'Η 'Αθήνα ἐλεύθερη. 'Ο ΕΛΑΣ ἀπελευθερωτής" [Athens is Free ELAS, the Liberator], *Avge*, 18.10.64 Reminiscences of I. Pyriochos, P. Kotsakes (Nestoras), K. Porphyres, S. Tsirkas, and others.

"'Η 'Εθνική 'Αντίσταση στήν 'Α. Μακεδονία καί Δ. Θράκη" [The National Resistance in Eastern Macedonia and W. Thrace], *Avge*, 24.7.–7.8.60. /1,2,L/

'Η μαύρη βίβλος τῶν βουλγαρικῶν ἐγκλημάτων εἰς τήν 'Αν. Μακεδονίαν καί Δυτ. Θράκην 1941–1944 [The Black Book of Bulgarian Crimes in Eastern Macedonia and Western Thrace 1941–1944]. Edited by a committee of professors of the Universities of Athens and Thessaloniki: D. Chondros, I. Theodorakopoulos, N. Vlachos, S. Kyriakides, Ch. Phrangkistas (Athens, 1945).

'Ημέρα μνήμης τῶν 'Ισραηλιτῶν θυμάτων τοῦ Ναζισμοῦ [Memorial Day for the Jewish Victims of Nazism]. Edited by the Jewish Community of Athens (Athens, 1963).

"'Η πραγματική ἱστορία τοῦ ἀνταρτοπολέμου" [The Real History of the Guerrilla War], *Anexartetos Typos*, 4.7.60.–1961. A moderate account by a group of anonymous authors, based on their reminiscences and some "resistance archives."

Herzog, Robert. *Grundzüge der deutschen Besatzungsverwaltung in den ost—und südosteuropäischen Ländern während des zweiten Weltkrieges* (Tübingen, 1955). / 3,7,8 /

Hillgrubber, Andreas. *Südost-Europa im Zweiten Weltkrieg. Literaturbericht und Bibliographie* (Frankfurt/M., 1962). A useful catalog of standard literature on South East Europe during World War II. However, the titles referring to Greece must be used with some caution, since they were apparently not compiled by an informed scholar. Beside repeated errors in spelling, etc., the book includes several unrelated works, even on ancient Greece and on "1821" (e.g., the memoirs of General Makrygiannes).

Οἱ Αἰγυπτιῶται εἰς τάς ἐπάλξεις: Ἡ συμβολή τοῦ Αἰγυπτιώτου Ἑλληνισμοῦ εἰς τόν ἐθνικόν ἀγῶνα 1940–1945 [The Egyptian Greeks at the Ramparts: The Contribution of the Greeks of Egypt to the National Struggle, 1940–1945]. Edited by the newspaper *Anatole* (Alexandria, 1946).

Οἱ ἀντάρτες τῆς XIII μεραρχίας τῆς Ρούμελης [The Guerrillas of the 13th Division of Roumele]. Edited by the 13th ELAS-Division. (n.p., 1945). A memorial edition containing many photographs.

"Οἱ ξένες ἐπεμβάσεις στήν ἐθνική μας ζωή" [Foreign Interventions in Our National Life], *Elefthere Hellada* (Rome), 18.2.–10.6.71. /7,L/

Hondros, John L. "The German Occupation of Greece, 1941–1944." Unpublished Ph.D. Dissertation, Vanderbilt University, 1969. This work relies on a good portion of German records and on a considerable stock of published material. In spite of incidental errors, the author clearly surpasses previous studies on the same subject; e.g., he was the first to disclose the real extent of Zervas' (EDES's) collaboration, or at least "contacts" with the Germans. This sensible account is soon to be published by Pella, New York.

Hourmouzios, Stelio. *No Ordinary Crown. A Biography of King Paul of the Hellenes* (London, 1972). /4,7,R/ No ordinary hymn . . .

Howard, Michael. *Grand Strategy.* Vol. IV (London: HMSO, 1972). Some scattered references to Greece. Much material on the "Second Front" dispute.

Hull, Cordell. *The Memoirs.* Vol. II (New York, 1948). Particularly interesting is the chapter referring to Anglo-Soviet negotiations for "spheres of influence" in the Balkans, and to the grumbling U.S. reaction.

Husemann, Friedrich. *Die guten Glaubens waren.* Vol. II: 1943–45 (Osnabrück: Munin, 1973). /2,3,6,7,R/ Extenuating history of the 4th SS-Division. Some chapters deal with its stay in Greece and anti-guerrilla operations.

Iatrides, John O. *Revolt in Athens. The Greek Communist "Second Round," 1944–1945* (Princeton, N.J.: Princeton University Press, 1972). Greek edition: (Athens: Nea Synora, 1973). /1,2,4,7/ A balanced and valuable account without ideological blinkers; the first to make extensive use of American unpublished materials. The author rejects the simple and "popular" plot theories of both sides. The work is strongest on the period immediately preceding and following the liberation, and somewhat weaker in its coverage of the occupation years.

———. "United States' Attitudes towards Greece during World War II" in Louisa Laourda, ed., *Μελετήματα στή μνήμη τοῦ Βασιλείου Λαούρδα* [Essays in Memory of Basil Laourdas] (Thessaloniki, 1975), 599–625.

———. "Greece and the Origins of the Cold War" in John T. A. Koumoulides, ed., *Greece in Transition* (London: Zeno, 1977), 236–251. /7/

———. "From Liberation to Civil War: The United States and Greece, 1944–46," *Southeastern Europe,* vol 3, 1 (1976), 32–43.

———, ed. *Ambassador MacVeagh Reports. Greece, 1933–1947* (Princeton, N.J.: Princeton University Press, 1980). Extensive reproduction of the American ambassador's wartime diary, correspondence, and diplomatic reporting. Particularly revealing on Greek affairs as perceived by the United States government.

Ioakeim, Metropolitan of Demetrias. *Μεταξύ κατακτητῶν καί ἀνταρτῶν* [Between Conquerors and Guerrillas]. (Athens, 1950). /1,2,3,5/ The author is not to be confused with the homonymous "Red Metropolitan" of EAM.

Ioannides, Yiannes. "'Αναμνήσεις καταγραμμένες ἀπό τόν 'Αλέκο Παπαπαναγιώτου: 'Από τήν 'Ακροναυπλία ὡς τόν Δεκέμβρη 1944" [Reminiscences recorded by Alekos Papapanagiotou: From Akronafplia until December 1944], *Avge,* 20.6.–22.8.76. Enlarged book edition *'Αναμνήσεις. Προβλήματα τῆς πολιτικῆς τοῦ ΚΚΕ στήν ἐθνική ἀντίσταση 1940–1945* [Reminiscences. Problems of the KKE Policy in the National Resistance 1940–1945], ed. A. Papapanagiotou (Athens: Themelio, 1979). /1,2,5,7,L/ Author was second ("organizational") secretary of KKE. His interesting tape-recorded apologia offers many valuable insights into the dimness surrounding party decisions, but is to be used with caution particularly on points concerning his own responsibility.

Ioannides, Yiannes. *Ἕλληνες καί ξένοι κατάσκοποι στήν 'Ελλάδα* [Greek and Foreign Spies in Greece] (Athens, 1952). /1,6/ The author provides an adventurous report on the achievements of his (espionage and sabotage) organization "Byrons." One serious fault of this work is the verbatim reproduction of two long passages from other sources (Gotses, Zalokostas) without any reference to them.

Ioannides, Yiannes. *'Ιάσων Καλαμπόκας. 'Ο θρυλικός ἥρωας.* [Iason Kalambokas. The Legendary Hero] (Athens, 1973). The hero's adventures during the Albanian campaign and the occupation. Not consulted.

Ioannidou-Lampea, Telesilla. *'Αγῶνες στό βωμό τοῦ καθήκοντος* [Struggles at the Altar of Duty] (Athens, 1960). /2,7,R/

Ioannou, L. "*Τό 'κίνημα' τοῦ Μάρτη 1943*" [The 'Coup' of March 1943], *Ethnike Antistase,* 4 (April 1963), 344–360. /4,6,L/

Ismay, Lord. *The Memoirs* (New York, 1960). /5,7/ Some references to Greece, particularly concerning the pros and cons of Churchill's pet idea regarding the capture of the Dodecanese in the summer and autumn of 1943.

Jecchinis, Chris. *Beyond Olympus. The Thrilling Story of the 'Train-busters' in Nazi-Occupied Greece.* Preface by C.M. Woodhouse (London: Harrap and Co., 1960) /1,2,5/ Greek youngster joins a British Military Mission and American sabotage detachment. Anti-EAM/ELAS source.

Joannides, E. *Bloody, But Unbowed. The Story of the Greek People's Struggle for Freedom* (London, 1949). /1,2,7/

Jones, Francis S. *Escape to Nowhere* (London, 1952).

———. *Hit or Miss* (London, 1954). Not very informative escape stories.

Jordan, William. *The Truth about Greece* (Melbourne, 1946). /2,6,R/ The author, a journalist and one of the first

BLOs, charges EAM with a regime of terror and Ares with a "sex and crime" record. In general, the pamphlet hardly does credit to its title.

———. "Fought Nazis and Reds for Freedom of Greeks." *Weekly News* (Auckland), 9.7.52.

———. *Conquest without Victory* (London and Auckland: Hodder and Stoughton, 1969). /2,5,7,R/ Foreword by C.M. Woodhouse. Less fanatical than the author's previous accounts cited above. Nevertheless, a source which should be used with caution. For example, the author accuses KKE/EAM of having denounced Woodhouse to the Gestapo during his clandestine visit to Athens (p.97). In reality it was the very communist leadership (Tzimas, Siantos) that organized Woodhouse's narrow escape. The latter (but unfortunately not in his foreword) and other BLOs (Myers, Edmonds) have fully appreciated this meritorious act of a political adversary.

K. *Γεώργιος Παπανδρέου. Ἡ ζωή του* [George Papandreou. His Life] (Athens, 1966). /7/ A flawless life—a usual biography.

K. [=Photiades, Kleanthes] "Τά γεγονότα στή Μέση 'Ανατολή" [The Events in the Middle East], *Rizospastes,* 2.3.75. /4,6,L/

Kabeli, Isaac. "The Resistance of the Greek Jews," *Yivo Annual of Jewish Social Science,* 8 (1953), 281–288. The ex-president of the Jewish community in Athens provides true but also occasionally fanciful details about Jewish exploits. He suppresses ELAS participation in the destruction of the Gorgopotamos bridge, e.g., and instead quotes "more than forty Jewish participants" among Zervas' (at best sixty) guerrillas.

Kailas, Metsos. *Ε.Λ.Α.Ν., 'Ελληνικό Λαϊκό 'Απελευθερωτικό Ναυτικό* [ELAN, Greek Peoples Liberation Navy] (Athens: Nea Vivlia, 1975). /2.L/

Kaimaras, Georgios D. *Ἱστορία τῆς 'Εθνικῆς 'Αντιστάσεως τοῦ 5/42 Συντάγματος Εὐζώνων Ψαρροῦ 1941–1944* [History of the National Resistance of Psarros' 5/42 Evzone Regiment, 1941–1944] (Athens, 1953). /2,6/ Author was one of the veterans in 5/42, earlier in the field than Psarros himself. Prejudiced and often unfair towards EAM/ELAS, but not to the extent of Dedouses (*supra*).

Kalambalikes, E.G. *Ἡ 'Εθνική 'Αντίστασις 1940–44 ζητᾶ δικαίωσιν* [The National Resistance 1940–44 Demands Vindication] (Athens, 1964). /2,6/ The author was one of the few outspoken anti-communist officers in ELAS.

Kalantzes, C. *Χρόνοι δουλείας. Οἱ σφαγές τῶν Καλαβρύτων* [Years of Slavery. The Slaughter at Kalavryta] (Athens, 1945). After a chronological introduction, the author deals in detail with the Kalavryta massacre, the worst (at least numerically) German reprisal in occupied Greece.

Kalatzes, Chrestos. "'Ιδεολογική ἐπιτομή τῆς νομοθεσίας τῆς 'Εθνικῆς 'Αντίστασης" [Ideological Summary of the Legislation of the National Resistance], *Epitheorese Technes,* 87–88 (March–April 1962), 366–375. /1,2,L/

Kalbe, Ernstgert. *Antifaschistischer Widerstand und volksdemokratische Revolution in Südosteuropa* (East Berlin: Verlag der Wissenschaften, 1974). /1,2,3,7,L/

Kaldires, D. and Nikolaides, P. *Ἡ πιό μαύρη ἡμέρα τῆς κατοχῆς* [The Darkest

Day of the Occupation] (Patras, 1963). The massacre at Kalavryta.

Kallinikides, Charalampos Ph. *Ἑλληνική Ἐθνική Ἀντίστασις (Αἷμα—Δάκρυ—Νίκη)* [Greek National Resistance (Blood—Tears—Victory)] (Thessaloniki, 1961). /1,2,R/ Extols the activities of PAO and other nationalist groups in Macedonia, condemning Bulgarians and "EAM-Bulgars."

Kalogiannes, Stavros. *Ἡμερολόγιο ἑνός στρατιώτου.* [Diary of a Soldier] (Athens, 1945). /1,5,7/ Impressions from occupied Athens, prisons, and concentration camps.

Kalvokoreses, Leones M. *Χρονικόν κατοχῆς τῆς Χίου παρά τῶν Γερμανῶν 1941–1944* [Chronicle of the Occupation of Chios by the Germans, 1941–1944] (Athens, 1958). /1,3,6/

Kanellopoulos, Panagiotes. *1935–1945. Ἕνας ἀπολογισμός* [1935–1945: An Account] (Athens, 1945). /1,4,5/

———. *Τά χρόνια τοῦ μεγάλου πολέμου. 1939–1944* [The Years of the Great War 1939–1944]. 2nd ed. (Athens, 1964). Based on his above-cited book, the former Vice-Premier and Minister in the Middle East provides a valuable account with more impartiality than most other political memoirs.

———. *Ἱστορικά δοκίμια* [Historical Essays] (Athens, 1975). Book edition of two series of articles. Especially the second series, dealing exclusively with the occupation years, fills some gaps in the earlier works. Moreover, the experience of 1967–74 seems to have induced Kanellopoulos to revise some of his earlier post-war convictions. A comparison with his papers dating from the Middle East years proves them to be nearer to the views contained in the "Essays."

Karabines, Demetres. *Μαζί μέ τόν ΕΛΑΣ* [Together with the ELAS] (Athens, 1946). /2,5,L/

Karachalios, Costas. *Νύχτες τῆς σκλαβωμένης Ἀθήνας* [Nights of Enslaved Athens] (Athens, 1946). /1,5/

Karagiannes, Georgios. *1940–1952. Τό δρᾶμα τῆς Ἑλλάδος—ἔπη καί ἀθλιότητες* [1940–1952. The Drama of Greece—Epics and Miseries] (n.p.,n.d. [=Athens, 1964]). /1,4,6,7,R/ Valuable (even if clearly biased) insider's information on the "loyalist" Greek scene of the Middle East.

Karagiannes, Yiannes V. *Ἡ προγραμένη Ἐθνική Ἀντίσταση* [The Proscribed National Resistance] (Athens, 1977). The author, one of the "proscribed" guerrilla veterans, accuses the post-war regimes of preference towards the former collaborators (and persecution of the resistance).

Karagiorgas, G. "Φῶς στή δολοφονία τοῦ Γιάννη Τσιγάντε" [Light on the Murder of Yiannes Tsigantes], *Ethnos,* 29.11.54–29.1.55.

———. "Ἡ τραγωδία τῆς Κεφαλληνίας." [The Tragedy of Cefallonia], *Ethnos,* 15.12.52–10.1.53. Deals with the massacre of the Italians in September 1943.

Karagiorgos, Costas. *Ἑλληνική Ἐθνική Ἀντίσταση 1941–1944. Ἡ Ρούμελι στίς φλόγες* [Greek National Resistance 1941–1944. Roumeli in Flames] (Athens, 1979)./2,6,L/ Much valuable information on the situation in Central Greece by the secretary of the KKE regional committee of Roumeli.

Karagitses, P. "Μία μεγάλη ἱστορική ἐπέτειος" [A Great Historical Anniversary], *Politike-Oikonomike Erevna,* (Sept. 1963), 24–26. A synopsis of the merits of EAM by an exmember of the KKE politburo.

Karales, Costas Th. *Ἱστορία τῶν δραματικῶν γεγονότων Πελοποννήσου 1943–1949* [History of the Dramatic Events in the Peloponnesus 1943–1949]. 2 vols. (Athens, 1958/1967). /R/

Karamouzes, Yiannes. *Πατριῶτες καί προδότες στό Μωρηᾶ* [Patriots and Traitors in the Peloponnesus] (Tripolis, 1950). /1,2,6,R/

Karas, S. "'Επανάσταση & *ἀντεπανάσταση στήν 'Ελλάδα* 1943–45" [Revolution and Counterrevolution in Greece, 1943–45], *Kommounistike Theoria kai Politike,* 25 (Oct.–Nov. 1978), 87–112. An estimation of KKE strategy connected with a critique of Partsalides' book (*infra*).

Karasoules, Panagiotes. "'Η ἐγκατάσταση στή Χίο τοῦ Ι. Καλαμπόκα καί βομβαρδισμός τοῦ '*Βίριλ*' " [The settlement of I. Kalambokas in Chios and the Bombing of the 'Viril'], *Chiake Epitheorese,* XII:34 (Feb. 1974). New information on the sinking of the Swedish supply ship 'Viril' by allied bombers.

Kartales, Georgios A. *Τά πεπραγμένα 1940–1944* [What Has Been Done, 1940–1944] (Athens, 1945). /1,2,6/ This largely autobiographic account provides much material about EKKA and its continuous conflict with EAM.

Kasapes, Vangeles (Kriton). *Στόν κόρφο τῆς Γκύμπρενας. Χρονικό τῆς 'Εθνικῆς 'Αντίστασης στόν Ἔβρο* [Inside Gymbrena. Chronicle of the National Resistance in the Evros region]. 2 vols. (Athens: Kalvos, 1977). /1,2,6,L/

Kasimates, Ioannis P. *'Απώ τήν παλαιά καί σύγχρονη Κυθηραϊκή ζωή* [Pages from the Old and Contemporary Life of Cythera] (Athens, 1957). /2,3,7/ Contains a chapter on the Italo-German occupation as well as a (critical) description of local EAM-ELAS activities.

Kastanes, Georgios I. *'Η ἐποποιΐα τῆς 'Ελλάδος, 1940–1944* [The Epic of Greece, 1940–1944] (Athens, 1948). /1,6,7,R/ The author writes in his capacity as chief of the self-styled "most important" resistance organization "National Directorate of Greek Fighters." Contains some information on (mostly) nationalist activities and German repressive measures.

Kästner, Erhart. *Ölberge, Weinberge* (Frankfurt and Hamburg, 1960). This valuable literary work provides candid war and post-war impressions of Greece.

Kastrinos, A. "'Η λαϊκή δικαιοσύνη καί αὐτοδιοίκησις εἰς τήν 'Ελεύθερη 'Ελλάδα 1941–45" [People's Justice and Self-Government in Free Greece 1941–45], *Historike Epitheoresis,* 1 (n.d. [=1963]), 132–160; 2 (Nov. 1963), 96–141. /1,6,L/ In spite of incidental errors, an essential source.

Kataphygiotes, Lambros K. *Οἱ ἀντάρται* [The Guerrillas] (Volos, 1946). /2,6,R/

Katsimangles, Georg. P. and Melas, N.G. *Τά πεπραγμένα καί ὁ ἀπολογισμός μας ἀπό 19.7.1941–6.2.1945* [Our Account of Activities from 19.7.1941–6.2.1945] (Athens, 1946). /1,3,6 / The principals of the Kallithea local administration deny any collaboration charges, and refer to their "patriotic exploits." Many pertinent documents.

Katsimbas, Giorgos. *Ὅταν ὁ ἄνθρωπος ραπίζεται* [When Man Gets Slapped] (Athens, 1966). /1,2,3,6/ One of the first ELAS officers (and a post-war deputy of EDA) attempts a noteworthy two-fold settlement of accounts: with the triumphant right and with the "orthodox" left.

Kavvadias, Epameinondas P. *Ὁ ναυτικός πόλεμος 1940–43 ὅπως τόν ἔζησα* [The Naval War 1940–43 as I Lived It] (Athens, 1950). /4,5,R/ This work was originally published in instalments in *Akropolis,* 25.12.49–14.7.50. The author—fleet commander, then Under-Secretary of the Navy—provides, apart from naval history, much (one-sided) information about the political entanglements of the period.

Kavvadias, K. P. *Δύσκολα Χρόνια* [Difficult Years] (Athens, 1950). Not consulted.

Kay, R.L. *Long-Range Desert Group in the Mediterranean* (Wellington: Department of Internal Affairs, 1950). Interesting account of commando raids.

Kazakos, Giorgos. *Ἄη Στράτης* [Saint Eustratios] (Athens: *Synchrone Epoche,* 1978). /1,3,5,7,L/ Reminiscences from exile until the escape from the island of St. Eustratios in June 1943.

Kedros, André. *La Résistance Grecque, 1940–1944* (Paris: Laffont, 1966). Greek edition: 2 vols. (Athens: Themelio, 1976). /L/ A number of errors remain in the amended Greek edition despite the corrections sent to the author by former protagonists. It is also particularly unfortunate that Kedros has repeated once more the traditionally inflated (and naturally more "popular") figures concerning the exploits of the Resistance—even though he has consulted some Wehrmacht records, and should therefore know the real German losses, at least in some instances.

Kelaides, Emmanuel. *Ἀναμνήσεις ἀπό τήν ἀεροπορία. Ἡ συμμετοχή της εἰς τούς ἐθνικούς ἀγῶνας 1924–1954.* [Reminiscences from the Air Force. Its Participation in the National Struggles 1924–1954] (Athens, 1972). Supplement under the same title: (Athens, 1973). /2.4.5.7/ The pertinent chapters deal with the author's mission to occupied Crete.

Kempner, Robert M. *Eichmann und Komplizen* (Zürich, 1961). The chapter concerning Greek Jewry contains an interesting letter by nuncio Roncalli (the subsequent Johannes XXIII) to ambassador Altenburg, expressing his appreciation for the latter's efforts on behalf of occupied Greece.

[Kennedy, Robert M.]. *German Antiguerrilla Operations in the Balkans 1941–1944* [(Washington, D.C.: Dept. of the Army, 1954). This very useful study is based on captured German records and monographs by leading German officers, prepared for the Historical Division of the U.S. Army. Unfortunately, the author presents a one-sided "German picture," disregarding nearly all Allied sources.

Kepeses, Nik. "Ἡ μάχη τῆς Ἠλεκτρικῆς" [The Battle of the Power Plant], *Ethnike Antistase,* 19, (June 1979), 33–37. /1,2,6,L/ An account of the disputed battle to save the main power station during the German evacuation of Athens.

Kitsikis, Dimitri. "La famine en Grèce (1941–1942). Les conséquences politiques." *Revue d'Histoire de la Deuxième Guerre Mondiale,* 74 (April 1969), 17–41.

Kitsios, Chr. "*Ἀπό τήν ἀντίσταση στήν Ἀνατολική Μακεδονία-Θράκη*" [From the Resistance in Eastern Macedonia and Thrace], *Ethnike Antistase,* 6 (Dec. 1963), 622–632. /1,2,6,L/

Kladakes, Markos. Letter in *Anexartetos Typos,* 19.9.–26.9.60. The author, a republican officer and initially a member of the ELAS Central Committee, provides useful information about the reasons and consequences of his escape to the Middle East.

Klien, Günther. "Partisanenkampf im Kriegsrecht." Unpublished LL.D. Dissertation, Hamburg University, 1953. /2,3,7/ The author argues that most German reprisals in Greece are justified by international law (including Kalavryta, but not the "events of Klissoura and Distomo").

Kobylinski, Hanna. *Den grekiska krisen* (Stockholm, 1945).

Koch, Gerhard. "Uber die griechische Widerstandsbewegung während des zweiten Weltkrieges und die Rolle deutscher Antifaschisten." *Wissenschaftliche Zeitschrift des Pädagogischen Instituts Erfurt,* I:1 (1964), 79–86. /1,2,3,6,L/

Kodros [=Ach. Kyrou]. *'Ο βασιλεύς εἰς τόν 'Αγῶνα* [The King in the Struggle] (Athens, 1945). And an enlarged edition, next entry.

———. *'Ο νικητής βασιλεύς* [The Victorious King] (Athens, 1946). /4,R/ Both books contain speeches and declarations by George II and some panegyric connecting text by the author.

Kofos, Evangelos. *Nationalism and Communism in Macedonia* (Thessaloniki: Institute for Balkan Studies, 1964). /7,8/ Best existing source for this ticklish subject.

Kokkinakes, D.I. " Ἕλληνες σαμποτέρ στά χρόνια τῆς κατοχῆς" [Greek Saboteurs during the Occupation Years], *Akropolis,* 18.7.–28.8.71.

———. " Ἕλληνες σαμποτέρ καί κατάσκοποι ἐναντίον τοῦ Γ' Ράϊχ" [Greek Saboteurs and Spies against the Third Reich], *Akropolis,* 7.11.71–13.2.72. /1,6/

Koligiannes, Costas. "Der Leninismus und die Historischen Erfahrungen der Kommunistis Partei Griechenlands." *Probleme des Friedens und des Sozialismus,* (1970), 475–482.

Kollias, Sephes, G. *'Αρχιεπίσκοπος ἀντιβασιλεύς Δαμασκηνός ὁ ἀπό Κορυνθίας. Μιά ἀνεπανάληπτη ἐκκλησιαστική μορφή* [Archbishop and Regent Damaskinos of Corinth. A Unique Ecclesiastical Figure]. 3rd ed. (Athens: Hiera Mone Petrake, 1975).

Kommission der Historiker der DDR und der UdSSR, ed. *Der deutsche Imperialismus und der zweite Weltkrieg.* Vol. IV (East Berlin, 1960). /1,2,3,7,L/

Konomos, Dinos. *'Η Ἑπτάνησος κατά τήν 'Ιταλική κατοχή (1941–1943).* [The Ionian Islands during the Italian Occupation (1941–1943)] (Athens, 1962). /1,2,3/

Konstantaras, C. *'Αγῶνες καί διωγμοί* [Struggles and Persecutions] (Athens, 1964). /1,2,5,L/ The author was a leading ELAS officer in Eastern Macedonia and Thrace, and provides the most objective description for this region. His account is clear and frank about internal problems of ELAS and related organizations.

Konstas, P.E. *'Η 'Ελλάς τῆς δεκαετίας 1940–50* [Greece during the Decade 1940–50] (Athens, 1955). /1,4,6,R/

Kontostanos, Methodios. *'Αρχεῖον καί καθημερινά γεγονότα ἐπί ἰταλικῆς καί γερμανικῆς κατοχῆς* [Archive and Daily Incidents during the Italian and German Occupations] (Corfu, 1949). The author was metropolitan of Corfu and served as mediator between the civilian population and the occupation authorities.

Kossyvakes, Nikephoros G. *'Η ὑπόθεσις Ν. Ζέρβα—'Εδ. Φερλάτου—Γρ. Κοσσυβάκη κατά τήν περίοδο τῆς 'Εθνικῆς 'Αντιστάσεως 1942–1945* [The Case of N. Zervas—Ed. Ferlato—

Gr. Kossyvakes during the Period of National Resistance 1942–1945] (Athens, 1963). /2,3,6/ A former EDES andarte accuses Zervas of collaboration, black-marketeering and even murder.

Kotsaridas, El. "'Ο Γεώργιος Παπανδρέου ἱστορεῖ: *Ἡ ἀνέμακτος ἀπελευθέρωσις*" [George Papandreou Speaks: The Bloodless Liberation], *Vema.* 11.–17.10.64.

Kotses, Spyros. *ΜΙΔΑΣ 614* [MIDAS 614] (Athens, 1976). /1,6 / The author, successor of I. Tsigantes as leader of "MIDAS 614," describes his own adventurous experiences and also offers good insights into the activities of some other secret organizations.

Kotzioulas, Georgios. *Ὅταν ἤμουν μέ τόν Ἄρη* [When I Was with Ares]. 3rd ed. (Athens: Themelio, 1965). /1,2,5,L/

———. *Θέατρο στό βουνό* [Theatre in the Mountains] (Athens: Themelio, 1976). /1,6,8,L/ Kotzioulas, friend of Ares and the principal playwright of EAM's Free Mountain Greece, offers a most fascinating report about this nearly unknown page of resistance history. Moreover, the book contains his fourteen extant plays recreating superbly life in the mountains. These plays, of more or less political character, were undoubtedly more effective than most EAM pamphlets.

Koukkides, K. *Ἡ δικαιοσύνη τους! Γερμανικά καί ἰταλικά στρατοδικεῖα κατοχῆς* [Their Justice! German and Italian Military Courts during the Occupation] (Athens, 1947). /1,3,6/

Kourmoules, Michales. *Ἡ λευκή ἐπανάσταση* [The White Revolution] (Athens, 1945). /1,5/

Kousoulas, Demetrios G. *The Price of Freedom. Greece in World Affairs, 1939–1953* (Syracuse, 1953).

———. *Revolution and Defeat. The Story of the Greek Communist Party.* Foreword by C.M. Woodhouse. (London, 1965). /R/ Better informed than the author's earlier book. However, his strong anti-communist bias leaves its unmistakable stamp on the narrative and—in spite of the sometimes deceptive "impartiality"—he provides more ideology than history.

———. *Modern Greece: Profile of a Nation* (New York: Charles Scribner's Sons, 1974). /7,R/

Koutsogiannopoulos, Ch. Letter in *Akropolis,* 1.12.49. The leader of the secret organization "Prometheus II" denies Zervas' version of the EDES establishment in the mountains.

Koutsoumes, Dinos. *4 χρόνια ἄγνωστη Ἑλληνική ἱστορία* [Four Years of Unknown Greek History] (Alexandria, 1946). /4,6/

Kritsikis, Katharina. "Der Anteil deutscher Antifaschisten am Widerstandskampf des griechischen Volkes im sweiten Weltkrieg." Unpublished Ph.D Dissertation, Rostock University, 1971. Not consulted.

Kühnrich, Heinz. *Der Partisanenkrieg in Europa 1939–1945. ([East] Berlin: Dietz, 1965). /2,7,L/*

———. "Biographische Skizzen: '. . . weil ich meiner Idee treu geblieben bin.' Werner Illmer." *Beiträge zur Geschichte der Arbeiterbewegung,* 19 (1977), 105–109. Deals with the cooperation of German communists and EAM/ELAS.

Kyriakides, G. "Τά αἴτια τῆς ἥτας τοῦ κινήματος." [The Reasons for the Defeat of the Movement], *Avge* 3.4.77. The author denies Russian responsibility for the defeat of EAM-KKE, and in particular the truth of the "horrible" accusation (made even by communists) that Stalin had "given the British the green light in Greece."

Kyrkos, L. *Τό KKE ἐσωτερικοῦ καί ἡ ἐθνική ἀντίσταση* [The KKE of the Interior and National Resistance] (Athens: KKE Interior, n.d.[= 1977]). A brochure covering the parliament debate of 25.8.1977 on the recognition of EAM as "national resistance."

Kyrou, Achil. A. *Σκλαβωμένοι νικηταί* [Enslaved Victors] (Athens, 1945). /1,6,R/

———. *Ἡ συνωμοσία ἐναντίον τῆς Μακεδονίας 1940–49* [The Conspiracy against Macedonia 1940–49] (Athens, 1950). Accuses EAM and KKE of traitorous collaboration with the Slavic neighboring states in order to deprive Greece of her northern provinces. See also under: Kodros.

Kyrou, Alexes Ad. *Ὄνειρα καί πραγματικότης. 45 χρόνια διπλωματικῆς ζωῆς* [Dreams and Reality. 45 Years of Diplomatic Life] (Athens, 1972). /1,5,7,R/

Lagares, Demetrios G. *Πέντε χρόνια αἵματος, δόξης καί σκλαβιᾶς. Ἡ Πάτρα στόν πόλεμο καί στήν κατοχή* [Five Years of Blood, Glory and Slavery. Patras during the War and the Occupation] (Patras, 1946). /1,2,3,6,R/

Lagdas, Panos. *Ἄρης Βελουχιώτης* [Ares Velouchiotes]. 2 vols. (Athens: Kypsele, 1964–65). /2,7,L/ Ample information about ELAS and its "archikapetanios," but also a typical example of the "hagiographical" style of most Greek biographies.

Lagios, Vasileios G. *Ἀλβανοί κι' ἀλβανική προπαγάνδα (1939–1944)* [Albanians and Albanian Propaganda (1939–1944)] (Athens, 1951). /7,R/ Deals with Albanian efforts to annex—allegedly with the help of the KKE—the adjoining part of Epirus, the Chamouria. The local minority, the Chams, are generally presented as criminal tools of Tirana. Their subsequent bloody persecution by EDES and "all true Greeks" is welcomed by the author who only regrets that the "dirty Albanian carcinoma" has not yet been totally eliminated.

Lambrinos, G. "Ἡ περίπτωση Ἄριστου Καμπάνη: *Τό πνεῦμα τοῦ δοσιλογισμοῦ*" [The Case of Aristos Kambanes: The Spirit of Collaborationism] *Rizospastes*, 7.10.47 and *Aiolika Grammata*, V: 29 (1975), 385–386.

Lambros, Chariton K. *Οἱ Τσάμηδες καί ἡ Τσαμουριά* [The Chams and the Chamouria] (Athens, 1949). Same subject as Lagios (*supra*).

Lanz, Hubert. *Gebirgsjäger. Die 1. Gebirgsdivision 1935–1945* (Bad Nauheim: Podzun, 1954). /3,6,7/

Lappas, Takes. *Ἡ σφαγή τοῦ Διστόμου* [The Slaughter at Distomo] (Athens, 1945).

Laternser, Hans. *Verteidigung deutscher Soldaten* (Bonn, 1950). Author defended some of the "South-East generals," tried by the U.S. Military Court on charges of having committed crimes in occupied Greece and Yugoslavia.

La trahison de Tito envers la Grèce Démocratique. KKE publication. (n.p., n.d.[= 1949] A collection of articles by Zachariades and others against the "Yugoslav traitors," secretly collaborating during the occupation and the civil war with the imperialistic enemies of KKE.

Lazitch, Branko. *Les Partis Communistes d'Europe 1919–1955* (Paris, 1956).

Lee, Arthur S. *The Royal House of Greece* (London and Melbourne, 1948). /4,6,7,R/

Leeper, Reginald. *When Greek Meets*

Greek (London and Toronto, 1950). /1,4,5/ Well-written memoirs of the ambassador to the Greek government-in-exile, but disappointingly little new material in view of the author's leading part in Greek affairs.

Levides, Al. "'Επτά ἡμέρες μέ τό ὄνειρον τῆς ἀπελευθερώσεως τῆς Δωδεκανήσου" [Seven Days Dreaming of the Liberation of the Dodecanese], *Naftike Hellas*, 215–218, (Sept.–Dec. 1951). /1,4,5/

Lefterias, T. [=Papadakes, Vangeles] and Chatzes, Thanases. "EAM: *Τό λαϊκό ἔπος πού χάθηκε* . . ." [EAM: The People's Epic Which Was Lost . . .], *Sosialistike Poreia*, 105–108 (Oct. 1977). /1,2,6,L/ An informative discussion chaired by A. Stangos.

Linardatos, Spyros. "Οἱ φοιτητές στήν ἀντίσταση" [The University Students in the Resistance], *Epitheorese Technes*, 87–88 (March–April 1962), 463–471. /1,6,L/

Lincoln, John. *Achilles and the Tortoise. An Eastern Aegean Exploit* (London, 1958). BLO of Samos (1944) reports on his simultaneous cordial contacts with Greek resistance and Italian occupation forces.

Lindström, Margit. *Grekland* (Stockholm, 1949). /7/

Livekos, Phrixos. *Τμίμι* [Tmimi]. 2nd ed. (Athens: Synchrone Epoche, 1977). /4,5,L/ Vivid impressions from service in the Middle East, the disarming of rebellious Greek units and the subsequent deportation of the "mutineers." Stresses the prevailing sense of solidarity that tried to overcome the cruel conditions in Tmimi and other African detention camps.

Lizardos, Spyr. N. *'Ιστορικόν καί συνέπειες τῆς ἀπεργίας τῆς 1ης 'Οκτωβρίου 1943* [History and Consequences of the Strike of October 1, 1943] (Athens, 1945). /1,3,5/

———. *Τό ἔγκλημά μου καί ἡ τιμωρία μου* [My Crime and My Punishment] (Athens, 1945). /1,3,5/ Ex-director of the gas works in Athens denies all charges of having collaborated with the occupation authorities and of having denounced strikers to them.

Lodwick, John. *The Filibusters. The Story of the Special Boat Service* (London, 1947). /1,4,6,7/ Report on commando raids in the Aegean.

Logothetopoulos, C. *'Ιδοῦ ἡ ἀλήθεια* [Here is the Truth] (Athens, 1948). /3,5,R/ Apologia by the occupation premier.

Lohmann, Walter and Hildebrand, Hans. *Die deutsche Kriegsmarine 1939–1945* (Bad Nauheim: Podzun, n.d.). /3,7,8/ Many data about German naval administration.

Louvares, Nikolaos I. "Κατοχή: *'Ο Γολγοθᾶς ἑνός ἔθνους*" [Occupation: The Golgotha of a Nation], *Ethnikos Keryx*, 2.4.–11.6.50. /1,3,5/ Informative and self-critical account by an (indeed) "involuntary" collaborator.

Loverdo, Costa de. *Les Maquis rouges des Balkans* (Paris: Stock, 1967).

———. *Le Bataillon Sacré 1942–1945* (Paris: Stock, 1968). /4,6/

Lykourezos, Panagiotes. *Μυστική 'Οργάνωσις* "Κόδρος" [Secret Organization Kodros'] (Athens, n.d. [=1965]). /1,5,R/

Macmillan, Harold. *The Blast of War, 1939–1945* (London: Macmillan, 1967). /2,4,5,7/ Valuable source for the British view of Greek affairs, particularly in 1944.

Makkas, Leon. *'Εθνικαί ἀγωνίαι καί προσδοκίαι (1937–1945)* [National Agonies and Expectations (1937–1945)] (Athens, 1945). /6,7 / Contains many political memoranda and similar documents.

Mamopoulos, Petros. *Μέρες ἀγωνίας* [Days of Agony] (Athens, 1949). /5/ Deals with the transition period after the German evacuation of the Peloponnesus.

Mangriotes, Demetrios I. *Θυσίαι τῆς Ἑλλάδος καί ἐγκλήματα κατοχῆς κατά τά ἔτη 1941–1944* [Sacrifices of Greece and Occupation Crimes During the Years 1941–1944] (Athens, 1949). /1,2,3/

Manousakas, Yiannes. *Χρονικό ἀπό τήν ἀντίσταση (μετά τήν Ἀκροναυπλία)* [Chronicle from the Resistance (after Akronafplia)] (Athens, Kapopoulos, 1976). /1,2,5,L/ A most graphic and frank memoir exposing and criticizing EAM-KKE "mistakes" at all levels of the organizational hierarchy, particularly those related to everyday human relations in "Free Mountain Greece." This latter dimension, most often absent from similar works, constitutes a rare asset that greatly enhances the general credibility of this book.

Manousakis, Gregor. *Hellas—Wohin? Das Verhältnis von Militär und Politik in Griechenland seit 1900* (Bad Godesberg, 1967). /R/

Marc, Leon [=Markantonatos, Leonidas]. *Les heures douloureuses de la Grèce Libérée. Journal d'un témoin (Octobre 1944–Janvier 1945)* (Paris, 1947). Some errors in the author's review of events preceding the winter of 1944.

Markares, Petros. "Πολιτικό θέατρο τοῦ λαοῦ στόν ἀγῶνα γιά τήν ἀπελευθέρωση" [People's Political Theatre in the Liberation Struggle], *Theatro*, IX: 53–54 (Sept.–Dec. 1976), 31–38. Same subject as Alexiou, Kotzioulas (*supra*).

Maroudes, Giorgos. *Τό ἡμερολόγιο τῆς πείνας.* [The Diary of Hunger] (Athens, Kedros, 1976). /1,5,L/ A moving account of the terrible winter of 1941–1942.

Matarasso, I.A. *Κι' ὅμως ὅλοι τους δέν πέθαναν . . .* [And Yet All of Them Did not Die . . .] (Athens, 1948). /3,6/ Report on the Sephardic Jewry of Thessaloniki.

Mathiopoulos, Basil P. *Die Geschichte der sozialen Frage und des Sozialismus in Griechenland (1821–1961)* (Hannover, 1961). /7/ Useful review, based on the author's dissertation.

———. *Ἡ Ἑλληνική Ἀντίσταση (1941–1944) καί οἱ "Σύμμαχοι" (ὅπως καταξιώνεται ἀπό τά ἐπίσημα γερμανικά ἀρχεῖα)* [The Greek Resistance (1941–1944) and the 'Allies' (as confirmed by the Official German Archives)], (Athens: Papazeses, 1976). Another presentation of many excerpts from German records, based on a series published in *Eleftheria* in 1960–1961. The author—as also Enepekides (*supra*)—undoubtedly has extended considerably the source basis for the Greek resistance; but unfortunately—again as in the latter—he reduces greatly the potential for scholarly use by omitting all fascicle numbers. According to the attached bibliography, the connecting text relies also on a good portion of pertinent literature, but apparently the author did not make thorough use of it. As a result, beside a number of errors, most of the "revelations" presented are either contrived or have long been known to be false. On the whole, this book neither reaches the scholarly reliability of the author's earlier study nor the usual standard of his journalistic work.

Matthews, Kenneth. *Memories of a*

Mountain War. Greece 1944–1949 (London: Logman, 1972)./2,4,5,7/

Mavrides, Chrys. *'Ηρωϊκά (17.8.1944)* [Heroics] (Athens, 1960). /1,3,5,L/ Dedicated to the bloody raid by German troops and collaborators into Kokkinia.

Mavromatis, Panajotis. "Der Beitrag des griechischen Volkes zum antifaschistischen Freiheitskampf." In Kommission . . . (*supra*) IV, 245–254. /1,3,L/

Maximos, S. *Ποῦ βαδίζουμε* [Where Are We Going]. 2nd ed. (Athens, 1945). /5,L/ The prominent communist provides valuable information about his negotiations with the bourgeois parties.

Mazarakes-Ainian, Alexandros. *'Απομνημονεύματα* [Memoirs] (Athens, 1948). This informative account (largely in diary form) offers a good example of the dislike of resistance, present even amongst the most anti-German Greek generals.

"Μαζί μέ Γερμανούς ἐξώντωναν Ἕλληνες" [Together with Germans They Exterminated Greeks], *Eleftheria*, 24.1.–6.2.65. /1,3,6/ Deals with the collaborating Macedonian group EES, which after the war posed—rather successfully—as a "resistance organization."

McGlynn, M.B. *Special Service in Greece* (Wellington: Dept. on Internal Affairs, 1953). /2,6/ Extols the achievements of some BLOs from New Zealand.

McNeill, William H. *The Greek Dilemma. War and Aftermath* (London, 1947). /6,7/ This objective first-hand account of the period after the liberation is repeatedly misinformed about earlier events.

Medlicott, W.N. *The Economic Blockade*. Vol. II (London: HMSO, 1959). Presents the official British view, disregarding German, Swedish, and (most) American sources on this controversial subject.

Melas, Michael K. *'Αναμνήσεις ἑνός πρέσβεως* [Recollections of an Ambassador] (Athens, 1967). /7/ The pertinent chapters contain information on Melas' mostly humanitarian activities in London and Switzerland during the war years.

Menasseh, Alvertos. *Birkenau (Auschwitz II). 'Αναμνήσεις ἑνός αὐτόπτου μάρτυρος. Πῶς ἐχάθηκαν 72.000 'Εβραῖοι* [Birkenau (Auschwitz II). Recollections of an Eyewitness. How 72,000 Greek Jews Perished] (Thessaloniki: Israelian Community, 1974). /1,3,5/ Nightmarish reminiscences covering the deportation from Thessaloniki and life in various concentration camps, in particular Birkenau and Dachau.

Mercouri, Melina. *Ich bin als Griechin geboren* (Berlin: Blanvalet, 1971). /5,7/ Reminiscences on the actress's development of political consciousness during the occupation years.

Metsopoulos, Thanases (Stavros). *Στά Μακεδονικά βουνά. Τό 30° Σύνταγμα τοῦ ΕΛΑΣ* [In the Macedonian Mountains. The 30th Regiment of ELAS] (Génève: Editex, 1971); 2nd slightly enlarged ed.: (Athens: Kedros, 1979). /2,5,L/ The political adviser (kathodegetes) of the regiment provides an informative and often self-critical account. One of the most candid communist memoirs.

Metzsch, Friedrich-August von. *Die Geschichte der 22. Infanterie-Division 1939–1945* (Kiel, 1952). /3,6,7/

Mexes, Demos N. "'Η αὐτοδιοίκηση στήν ἐλεύθερη 'Ελλάδα τῆς κατοχῆς." [Self-Government in Free

Greece during the Occupation], *Anti* 22.3.75, 8–10.

Meynaud, Jean. *Les forces politiques en Grèce* (Montreal, 1965). Includes a useful, but somewhat simplifying review of the occupation.

Mezevires, G. *Τέσσαρες δεκαετηρίδες εἰς τὴν ὑπηρεσίαν τοῦ Β. Ναυτικοῦ* [Four Decades in the Service of the Royal Navy] (Athens, 1971). /4,5,7,R/

Michos, Dem. "Τό ἀντάρτικο στό Μωριά" [The Guerrilla Movement in the Peloponnesus], *Historikon Archeion Ethnikes Antistaseos,* Nos. 4; 5–6; 7–8; 10–11 (1958–1959). /2,6,L/

Milliex, Roger. *Les Universitaires et Intellectuels de Grèce au service de la Résistance* (Paris, 1945).

———. *A l'Ecole du Peuple Grec 1940–1944* (Vichy, 1946). Two impressive accounts written by a friend of Greece.

Molho, Michael, ed. *In Memoriam. Hommage aux victimes juives des Nazis en Gréce.* 2 vols. (Thessaloniki, 1948). /3,6,8/ In spite of its errors and its understandable partiality, the only comprehensive work about the destruction of Greek Jewry.

Moraites, Andreas. "'Η 'Επιμελητεία τοῦ 'Αντάρτη" [The Guerrilla Commissariat], *Historikon Archeion Ethnikes Antistaseos,* Nos. 4; 5–6; 7–8; 9; 12–13 (1958–1959). /1,2,6,L/ Valuable material on the work of the ELAS supply department by its former principal.

Moraites, L. *'Από τ'ἀντάρτικο τῆς Ρούμελης* [From the Guerrillas of Roumele] (Athens, 1946). /2,5,L/

Morrell, Sydney. *Spheres of Influence.* 2nd ed. (New York, 1971). /7/ Provides good background material on Greece. However, the author's version of the civil war, as largely due to the previous strongly pro-EAM attitude of the British, is highly contestable.

Moscardelli, Giuseppe. *Cefalonia* (Rome, 1945). /3,6 / Same subject as Formato (*supra*).

Moss, Stanley W. *Ill-Met by Moonlight* (New York, 1950). /2,4,5/ Diary-based report by one of the two British officers who kidnapped the German general Kreipe from occupied Crete, thanks to the indispensable help of the local resistance and the civilian population. This aspect is somewhat neglected in other accounts.

———. *A War of Shadows* (London and New York, 1952). /2,3,4,5/ Description of the author's subsequent activities in Crete and Macedonia—always in the face of interference by EAM/ ELAS.

Moutouses, Nikolaos Ch. *Καί διηγῶντας τα νά κλαῖς . . . Ἔξη μῆνες αἰχμάλωτος τοῦ Ἄρη Βελουχιώτη* [And Telling it, You Cry . . . Six Months Captive of Ares Velouchiotes]. 2nd ed. (Athens, 1959). /2,5,R/

Mulgan, John. *Report on Experience.* (London, 1947). /1,2,5/ Witty memoir by a BLO, fully appreciating the blameless—and truly heroic—attitude of the mountain population.

Myers E.C.W. *Greek Entanglement* (London: Hart-Davies, 1955). Greek edition: (Athens: Exantas, 1976). /1,2,4,5,8/ Author was first commander of the British Military Mission to the Greek guerrillas. His memoir—indispensable for resistance history—was written in 1945, but publication was blocked for a decade, due to its inherent criticism of official British policy. However, Myers seems to apply his final views on Greek affairs (as they had developed by the summer of 1943) to the preceding period as well.

As a result, he provides little information about his previous very sharp anti-EAM policy recommendations—vetoed only by his Cairo superiors and documented many times in British records of the spring of 1943. Neither does he mention his general dislike of the "Asiatic" and "untrustworthy" Greek people.

———. "The Andarte Delegation to Cairo: August, 1943" in Phyllis Auty and Richard Clogg, eds, *British Policy . . .*, 147–166. /2,4,5/

Myridakes, Michael I. *'Αγῶνες τῆς φυλῆς.—'Η ἐθνική ἀντίστασις ΕΔΕΣ-ΕΟΕΑ 1941–1944* [The Struggle of the Race. The National Resistance EDES-EOEA 1941–1944] (Athens, 1948); 2nd enlarged ed.: (Athens: Sideres, 1977). /2,6,R/ Author was adjutant of Zervas and feels still duty bound.

Myrsiades, Costas. "Yiannis Ritsos and Greek Resistance Poetry," *Journal of the Hellenic Diaspora*, V:3 (1978) 47–56.

Naltsas, Christophoros A. *Τό Μακεδονικόν ζήτημα καί ἡ Σοβιετική πολιτική* [The Macedonian Question and Soviet Policy] (Thessaloniki, 1954). /1,2,6,7,R/ The chief of the political branch of PAO provides much material on the merits of his organization, and on the "treasonable" misdeeds of KKE/EAM/ELAS during the Occupation. Naltsas presents many "secret agreements" of KKE/EAM/ELAS with the Bulgarians, Germans, etc., the alleged texts of which fell into PAO's hands with remarkable regularity. Most of these fakes (fabricated as early as 1943–44) are of very poor quality, but nevertheless have been reproduced in the bulk of the "nationalist" literature.

Nathenas, Andreas E. *Ἄγνωστοι πτυχαί τῆς 'Εθνικῆς 'Αντιστάσεως, 1941–1945* [Unknown Aspects of the National Resistance 1941–1945] (Athens, 1978). /2,4,5,7,R/ Reminiscences and documents concerning the author's activities in Athens, Middle East, and Crete.

Nekrich, A. " 'The Balkan Alternative,' " *International Affairs* (Moscow), 8 (1959), 66–72.

Nenedakes, A. *'Ο Ζωγράφος Τσίγκος στόν πόλεμο καί στή φυλακή* [The Painter Tsingos in War and in Prison] (Athens, 1965). /4,5,L/ Deals with Tsingos (famous painter and leftist officer) and with his role during the "anomalies" in the Middle East. A sensitive first-hand account.

Nepheloudes, Pavlos. *Στίς πηγές τῆς κακοδαιμονίας. Τά βαθύτερα αἴτια τῆς διάσπασης τοῦ ΚΚΕ 1918–1968* [At the Sources of Misfortune. The Deeper Causes of the KKE Split, 1918–1968] (Athens: Gutenberg, 1974). /1,6,7,L/ Contains a good, leftist review of occupation events.

Nepheloudes, Vassiles. *Ἕλληνες πολεμιστές στή Μέση 'Ανατολή* [Greek Warriors in the Middle East] (Athens, 1945). /4,6,L/ Much valuable but biased information on the mutiny of April 1944 and its antecedents.

Neubacher, Hermann. *Sonderauftrag Südost 1940–45* (Göttingen: Musterschmidt, 1956). /3,5,7/ Essential report by Hitler's plenipotentiary for the South East European countries. Most references to Greece deal with sundry efforts for a reduction of Greek inflation. Interesting, but only partially correct is his version of German negotiations with BLO Don Stott.

Nikoloudes, Theologos. *'Η Ἑλληνική Κρίσις* [The Greek Crisis]. 2nd ed.

(Cairo, 1945). /4,6,R/ Metaxas' exminister for propaganda nostalgically praises the "national" regime and denounces the subsequent "leftist" governments, especially the "internationalist" Kanellopoulos. The author also reproduces his memoranda to George II and Churchill.

Noel-Baker, Francis. *Greece. The Whole Story* (London, 1945).

O'Ballance, Edgar. *The Greek Civil War 1944–1949* (London, 1966). Contains a useful, but sometimes simplifying review of Greek resistance.

Olshausen, Klaus. *Zwischenspiel auf dem Balkan. (Die deutsche Politik gegenüber Jugoslawien und Griechenland von März bis Juli 1941)* (Stuttgart, 1973). /3,7,8/ Best existing source for the early part of the German occupation.

Önder, Zehra. *Die türkische Außenpolitik im 2. Weltkrieg* (Munich: Oldenbourg, 1977)./7/

Orestes [=Mountrichas, Andreas]. "Γιατί ὁ ΕΛΑΣ δέν κατέλαβε τήν 'Αθήνα" [Why ELAS Did not Seize Athens], *Athenaike*, 14.3.–30.4.55.

———. "'Από τά πρῶτα βήματα τοῦ ΕΑΜ στήν παντοδυναμία τοῦ ΕΛΑΣ" [From the First Steps of EAM to the Omnipotence of ELAS], *Akropolis*, 12.2.–11.11.61. Author was a communist veteran and one of the first ELAS "kapetanios" in the field. Soon after the "second round" (Dec. 1944), he left the KKE and finally became one of the favorite writers in conservative newspapers. His critical retrospective provides many particulars of ELAS's ups and downs, but his "journalistic duty" of producing sensations and his bias against the leadership of KKE (and partially that of ELAS) sometimes leads to conflicts with historical truth.

Oschlies, Wolf. *Bulgarien—Land ohne Antisemitismus* (Erlangen: Ner-Tamid, 1976). /7/ Refers also to the anti-Jewish measures in the Bulgarian occupation zone of Greece.

Pagtziloglou, Miltos. *Νύχτα καί καταχνιά. Διηγήματα καί μαρτυρίες ἀπό τήν 'Εθνική μας 'Αντίσταση 1941–1949* [Night and Fog. Accounts and Testimonies of our National Resistance 1941–1949] (Athens, 1979). /1,2,6,7,L/

Pallis, A.A. *Problems of Resistance in the Occupied Countries* (London 1947). /1,3/

Palmer, Stephen E., Jr. and King, Robert R. *Yugoslav Communism and the Macedonian Question* (Hamden, Conn.: Archon, 1971). /2,7,8/ This distinguished work contains some valuable information on Greek Macedonia (and the attitude of KKE).

Panhellenia Enosis Pathonton Opliton Chorophylakes [Panhellenic Union of Injured Gendarmes] *Κόκκινοι λύκοι. Τό χρονικόν τῆς ἀντεθνικῆς ἀνταρσίας.* [Red Wolves. The Chronicle of the Antinational Rebellion] (Athens, 1947). /2,3,7,R/ The contents and slant are implied in the title.

Panoutsopoulos, I. *Μία σελίς ἀπό τήν δράση τοῦ ΕΑΜ-ΕΛΑΣ στόν Μωρηᾶ* [One Page from the Action of EAM-ELAS in the Peloponnesus] (Athens, 1949). /2,5,R/

Panteleemon, Metropolitan [=Phostines]. *'Αγῶνες κάτω ἀπό τά δεσμά* [Struggle under the Chains] (Athens, 1946). /1,3,5,R/ Author organized "national" (anti-communist) resistance on Euboea, and had close contacts with Tsigantes' group.

Papadakes, V.P. *Διπλωματική 'Ιστορία τοῦ 'Ελληνικοῦ Πολέμου 1940–1945* [Diplomatic History of the Greek War

1940–1945] (Athens, 1956). /4,R/ The Metaxist author provides a great number of documents, but most of them are already known or of secondary importance. The selection criteria and the connecting text betray political prejudice. Unfortunately as yet the only existing "diplomatic history."

Papademetriou, Elle, ed. *'Ο κοινός λόγος. 'Αφηγήματα.* [The Common Word. Narratives] 2nd ed.: 3 vols. (Athens: Kedros 1972/1975). Vivid accounts by unnamed "simple" persons, many referring to occupation events.

Papademetriou, N. I. and Botses, Georgios A. *Γιατί ἡ 'Ελλάς ζητάει δικαιοσύνη* [Why Greece Asks for Justice] (Athens, 1946)./1,3/ Includes many pictures of starvation and reprisals by the occupation authorities.

Papadopoulos, Homeros I. *Τρία χρόνια—τρεῖς αἰῶνες* [Three Years—Three Centuries] (Athens, 1947). /1,5,R/

Papadopoulos, Panagiotes. *'Η ἐθνική ἀντίστασις κατά τῆς Βουλγαρικῆς ἐπιδρομῆς.* [The National Resistance against the Bulgarian Invasion] (Athens, 1953)./2,3,R/

Papaevgeniou, Athanasios *Μάρτυρες κληρικοί Μακεδονίας—Θράκης (1941–1945)* [Martyred Clergymen of Macedonia and Thrace (1941–1945)]. 2nd ed. (Athens, 1949). /R/

Papageorgiou, Constantine A. *Λυγγιάδες, τό χωριό ποῦ ρήμαξαν οἱ Γερμανοί . . . 3.10.43.* [Lyngiades, the Village the Germans Destroyed . . . 3 Oct. 1943] (Ioannina, 1947)

[Papagiannopoulos, Takes]. "Συνταγματάρχης Ψαρρός. *Σελίδες ἀπό τό ἡμερολόγιο ἑνός ἀντάρτου ὑπολοχαγοῦ*" [Colonel Psarros. Pages from the Diary of a Guerrilla Lieutenant], *Kathemerina Nea,* 16.9.45–12.1.46. /2,5,/ The author, Psarros' political adviser, was captured by ELAS in April 1944, tortured and finally "convinced" to convert. Nevertheless (or even therefore) this is the most balanced account concerning the fatal conflict between ELAS and EKKA (5/42 Rgt.).

Papagos, Alexander. "Guerillakrieg." In F.M. Osanka, ed., *Der Krieg aus dem Dunkel* (Cologne, 1963). /2,6,7,R/

Papaioannou, Apostolos (Metropolitan of Carpathos). *Τό χρονικόν τῆς 'Ιταλοκρατίας τῆς Ρόδου. 'Εγκαρτέρησις ἑνός λαοῦ* [The Chronicle of the Italian Rule in Rhodes. The perseverance of a People] (Athens, 1973). /1,6,7/

Papakongos, Costes. *Καπετάν Ἄρης. 'Ο ἀνταρτοπόλεμος στήν 'Ελλάδα 1940–45* [Kapetan Ares. The Guerrilla War in Greece, 1940–45] (Athens: Papazeses, 1976). /2,L/

———. *Γράμματα γιά τόν Ἄρη* [Letters About Ares] (Athens: Papazeses, 1976). /2,6,L/ The author asked former companions of Ares for written reminiscences. This book contains their answers and a commentary.

Papakonstantinou, Theoph. *'Ανατομία τῆς ἐπαναστάσεως* [Anatomy of the Revolution] (Athens, 1952). /7,R/ In his analysis of communist revolution, the excommunist author often quotes from KKE documents the allegedly treasonable passages only, separated from their context in a distorting manner.

Papakyriakopoulos, Io. P. *Βούλγαροι καί 'Ιταλοί ἐγκληματίαι πολέμου ἐν Μακεδονία* [Bulgarian and Italian War Criminals in Macedonia] (Athens, 1946). /1,3,6/ From the records of the first Greek trial of war criminals.

Papamanoles, Th. G. *Ρίμινι* [Rimini]

(Athens, 1945). /4,R/ Panegyric report in honor of the 3rd Mountain ("Rimini") Brigade.

———. *Κατακαϋμένη Ἤπειρος. Τό φρικτόν δράμα τῶν κατοίκων τῆς Θεσπρωτίας καί ἡ συνεργασία τῶν Ἀλβανῶν μετά τοῦ Ἄξονος 1940–1944* [Wretched Epirus. The Horrible Drama of the Thesprotian People and the Collaboration of the Albanians with the Axis, 1940–1944] (Athens, 1945). /1,2,3,R/

Papandreou, Andreas. *Democracy at Gunpoint* (London, 1970). Contains a broad review of occupation events. Some errors.

Papandreou, Georgios. *Ἡ ἀπελευθέρωσις τῆς Ἑλλάδος* [The Liberation of Greece] (Athens, 1945). /1,4,5/ The author provides, in chronological order, many of his documents (speeches, memoranda, letters) before and after his rise to the premiership. By means of these and scant connecting text, he identifies the steps of his own political career with progress towards liberation.

———. "Ἡ ἀπελευθέρωσις τῆς Ἑλλάδος" [The Liberation of Greece], *Kathemerina Nea,* 25.2.45 ff. Contains supplementary material not included in the book edition.

———. *The Third War* (Athens, 1948). A collection of articles dating from the civil war and partially reviewing the decisive year 1944 and the author's claim to have followed a specific and deliberate strategy.

Papapanagiotou, Alekos. "Προβλήματα τῆς ἱστορίας τῆς Ἐθνικῆς Ἀντίστασης" [Problems of the History of National Resistance], *Dialogos,* 9–10 (April 1974), 144–193. /1,L/

———. *Τό ΚΚΕ στόν πόλεμο καί στήν ἀντίσταση, 1940–1945* [The KKE in War and Resistance, 1940–1945] (Athens, 1974).

Papastephanou, Yiannes. "Ὑποκλοπή τηλεγραφικῆς συνδέσεως τόν καιρό τῆς κατοχῆς στή Χίο." [Tapping the Telegraph Connection in Chios during the Occupation], *Chiake Epitheorese,* XII:35 (June 1974), 107–110. /1,5/

Papasteriopoulos, Elias. *Ὁ Μωρηᾶς στά ὅπλα* [Peloponnesus in Arms]. 5 vols. (Athens, 1965/1975). /1,2,8,L/ A relatively moderate leftist work.

Papastrates, Prokopes. "British Foreign Policy towards Greece during the Second World War 1940–1945." Unpublished Ph.D. Dissertation, London University, 1978. Not consulted.

Papoulias, Karolos. "Ein Brevier griechischer Résistancegeschichte." In M. Nikolinakos and K. Nikolaou, eds. *Die verhinderte Demokratie: Modell Griechenland* (Frankfurt/M.: Suhrkamp, 1969), 101–118. Useful for broad background material on the resistance.

Paramythia. The Municipality of P. and the Society "The Friends of Souli," eds. *Μνήμη 49 προκρίτων Παραμυθιᾶς* [In Memoriam of 49 Notables of Paramythia] (Athens: Vivliotheke tou Genous, 1973). Dedicated to the memory of the notables, executed in 1943 by collaborating forces recruited from the Cham minority.

Partsalides, Metsos. *Διπλή ἀποκατάσταση τῆς Ἐθνικῆς Ἀντίστασης* [Double Rehabilitation of The National Resistance] (Athens: Themelio, 1978). /1,2,6,7,L/ Interesting analysis of KKE wartime strategy, especially concerning the critical year 1944, as seen from the author's vantage point as member of the KKE politburo and (since August 1944) secretary of EAM. His interpretation of various disputed points is remarkably outspoken; the frequent apologetic statements seem to be largely justified. Nevertheless, Partsalides' argumentation is, to great extent, based on long-known passages from other authors and fails to make use of information which is certainly accessible to the author. Exceptions to this certainly exist; the presentation of Zevgos' (heretofore unpublished) brief diary is the most notable one.

———. "'Η 'Ελληνική 'Εθνική 'Αντίσταση" [Greek National Resistance], *Neos Kosmos,* X VI: 11 (Nov. 1964), 1483–1494. /1,2,L/

———. "Στή μνήμη συκοφαντημένων κομμουνιστῶν" [In Memory of Slandered Communists], *Avge,* 27.–30.8.75. Refers mainly to Siantos, Karagiorges, and Ploumides.

———. "Οἱ ξένοι καί ἡ ἐθνική ἑνότητα" [The Foreigners and National Unity], *Avge* 26.9.76. Comments on an interview with Panagiotes Kanellopoulos.

———. "'Ορισμένες πλευρές τῆς σοβιετικῆς πολιτικῆς γιά τήν 'Ελλάδα" [Certain Aspects of the Soviet Policy towards Greece], *Avge* 3.4.77.

——— and Apostolou, Lefteres. "Τό 'Εαμικό κίνημα" [The EAM Movement], *Kommounistike Theoria kai Politike* 13 (Aug.–Sept. 1976), 28–33. The first and last secretary of EAM provide answers to three vital questions.

Passas, Ioannes D. *S.O.S.* (Athens, 1945). /1,2,7,R/

———. *Πῶς θά γίνη ὁ Τρίτος Γύρος* [How the Third Round Will Take Place] (Athens, 1945). Two extreme royalist pamphlets attacking republicans of all shades and "Bulgarian-controlled" EAM.

Patatzes, Soteres. *'Ιωάννης Σοφιανόπουλος* [Ioannes Sophianopoulos] (Athens, 1961).

———. *Ματωμένα χρόνια* [Bloody Years]. 2nd ed. (Athens: Yannikos, 1964). Well-written essays on events and characters of the resistance, and on consequent reprisals.

Pepones, Anastasios. *Προσωπική Μαρτυρία* [Personal Testimony] (Athens: Kedros, 1970). /1,5,8/ This sensitive work recreates superbly the tragic dilemma of liberal and moderate right-wing youth in occupied Athens. More sceptical than their extremist contemporaries, they were squeezed (and often absorbed) between an aggressive communist-dominated EPON and the "professional anti-communists" in the periphery of collaboration. Best account concerning student resistance, and one of the most remarkable books on the occupation generally.

Pepones, A. Ioannes. *Νικόλαος Πλαστήρας στά γεγονότα 1909–1945* [Nikolaos Plasteras in the Events 1909–1945]. Vol. II. (Athens, 1948). A biography of the usual kind, which contains some material on the occupation years, e.g., the general's famous letter to Tsouderos.

Perakakes, Nikos M. *'Η Κρήτη στίς φλόγες* [Crete in Flames] (Athens, 1975). /2,7/

———. *'Αφηγήσεις.* [Narratives] (Athens: Mylopotamos, 1977). /2,6,L/ The author compiled, among other information, a diary and various memoirs of outstanding Cretan guerrillas, members of ELAS in Crete or in the mainland.

Pesmazoglou, Georgios. I. *Τό χρονικόν τῆς ζωῆς μου (1889–1979).* [The Chronicle of my Life. (1889–1979)]. (Athens, 1979)./1,5,7/

Petrakes, E.L. *'Η 'Εθνική 'Οργάνωσις Κρήτης (ΕΟΚ) κατά τήν Γερμανικήν κατοχήν* [The National Organization of Crete (EOK) during the German Occupation] (Heraklion, 1953). /1,2,6,R/ Relies on the official report of EOK to the Greek General Staff.

Petropoulos, N.D. *'Αναμνήσεις καί σκέψεις ἑνός παλαιοῦ ναυτικοῦ* [Reminiscences and Thoughts of an Old Sailor]. Vol. IIIA/B: 1941–44. (Athens, 1971–72). Informative and sagacious account by a senior naval officer, who, starting from his professional vantage point, points out many reasons for subsequent Greek misfortunes. As to the "anomalies" in April 1944, he shows some critical impartiality which is traceable to his double (and thankless) role of official delegate and "involuntary mutineer." One of the best sources for the Greek scene in the Middle East.

Petsales, Thanases. *Τά δικά μας παιδιά. Χρονικό τῆς σκλαβιᾶς* [Our Children. Chronicle of Slavery] (Athens, 1946). /1,6,7/

Petsopoulos, Yiannes D. *Τά πραγματικά αἴτια τῆς διαγραφῆς μου ἀπό τό KKE* [The Causes for my Expulsion from the KKE] (Athens, 1946). /1,2,6,7,L/ This self-vindication by a veteran communist outsider repeatedly levels true as well as exaggerated charges against the war leadership of the KKE and EAM.

Petzopoulos, Th. *1941–1950: Τραγική πορεία* [1941–1950: Tragic Course] (Athens, 1953). /2,5,7,R/ Not very reliable account by an officer who successively served in EDES, Security Batallions, and the Royal Army.

Pharmakides, G.A. *Πεπραγμένα τῆς παρά τῷ πρωθυπουργῷ ὑπηρεσίας ἀνταποκρίσεων μετά τῶν γερμανικῶν ἀρχῶν κατά τήν κατοχήν* [Account of the Prime Minister's Liaison Office with the German Authorities during the Occupation] (Athens, 1957). /3,5/

Phloisvos, T. *Ὁ ΕΛΑΣ καί οἱ ἐθνοπροδότες στήν 'Ανατολική Μακεδονία* [The ELAS and the Traitors in Eastern Macedonia] (Kavalla, 1945). /1,2,L/

Phlountzes, Antones I. *Χαϊδάρι. Κάστρο καί βωμός τῆς ἐθνικῆς ἀντίστασης.* [Chaidari. Castle and Altar of the National Resistance] (Athens: Papazeses, 1976). /1,2,6,L/

———. *Στρατόπεδα Λάρισας-Τρικάλων (1941–1944). Ἡ γέννηση τοῦ ἀντάρτικου στή Θεσσαλία* [The Concentration Camps in Larisa and Trikala (1941–1944). The Birth of the Thessalian Guerrilla Movement] (Athens: Papazeses, 1978). /1,6,7,L/

———. *'Ακροναυπλία καί 'Ακροναυπλιῶτες.* [Akronafplia and the Akronafpliotes] (Athens, Themelio, 1979). /1,6,7,L/ As in his earlier works, the author gives again the "story" of the famous prison making use of his own recollections and other material. In this most recent book Phlountzes describes conditions in the "Marxist Academy" at Akronafplia both under the Metaxas regime and the occupation, to the bitter end. He acknowledges the sacrifice of those Akronafpliotes who were executed by the authorities as easily available hostages and the contribution to the resistance of those who managed to escape. The annexed lists of names identify surviving veterans.

Phokas, Demetrios G. *Ἔκθεσις ἐπί τῆς δράσεως τοῦ Β. Ναυτικοῦ κατά τόν πόλεμον 1940–1944* [Report on the Action of the Royal Navy during the War 1940–1944]. Vol. II (Athens, 1954). /4/

Official report by the Historical Department of the Greek Navy.

Phokas, Vasos. "'Ηρωϊκές μορφές στήν ἐθνική μας ἀντίσταση." [Heroic Figures in Our National Resistance], *Eptanesiaka Grammata,* 1–5 (Sept. 1950–Jan. 1951). /1/

Phokas-Kosmetatos, C.P. *'Η εἰσαγωγή τῆς ἰταλικῆς ἰονικῆς δραχμῆς εἰς τήν 'Επτάνησον (1941–1943)* [The Introduction of the Italian Ionian Drachma into the Ionian Islands (1941–1943)] (Athens, 1946). /3/

Phosterides, Antonios. *'Εθνική 'Αντίστασις κατά τῆς βουλγαρικῆς κατοχῆς 1941–45* [National Resistance Against the Bulgarian Occupation 1941–1945] (Thessaloniki, 1959). /2,6,R/ Account of resistance in East Macedonia written under the name of the leader of the nationalist bands Phosterides (="Tsaous Anton"). Contains many photographs and personal information on guerrillas.

Phylaktos, Demetres. *1941–1944. 'Εθνική 'Αντίσταση. 'Αναμνήσεις ἀπό τό Βελβεντό* [1941–1944. National Resistance. Reminiscences from Velvedo] (Athens, 1977). /1,2,6,L/

Φύση καί προορισμός τοῦ ΕΛΑΣ [Nature and Mission of ELAS] (Athens, 1946). /2,L/

Pipineles, Panagiotes. *Γεώργιος Β΄* [George II] (Athens, 1951). /4,6,R/ Another hagiographical biography, which nevertheless provides some useful information and hints.

———. "Τά πολιτικά καί διπλωματικά παρασκήνια μιᾶς δεκαπενταετίας 1933–1948" [Behind the Political and Diplomatic Scenes of Fifteen Years: 1933–1948] *Akropolis* 2.3.–15.8.58 /7,R/

Palsari, Ndreçi and Ballvora, Shyqri. *Historia e luftës antifashiste nacionalclirimtare të populit Shqiptar, 1939–1944* [History of the Antifascist National Liberation War of the Albanian People, 1939–1944. vol.I: April 1939–September 1943, edited by the Central Committee of the Albanian Communist Party, Institute of Marxist-Leninist Studies (Tirana, 1975). French edition: (Tirana, 1977). Scattered references to cooperation with the Greek resistance. Not consulted.

Ploumis, Demetrios A. *'Ο Γολγοθᾶς τοῦ ἔθνος. Οἱ μαῦρες ἡμέρες τῆς σκλαβιᾶς 1941–1944, στή Ρούμελη καί στό στοιχιομένο Χαϊδάρι.* [The Golgotha of the Nation. The Black Days of Slavery 1941–1944, in Roumeli and at Haunted Chaidari] (Athens, 1971). /2,3,5,R/ Reminiscences by the EDES chief for Western Roumeli, containing numerous documents and letters by himself, Zervas, Psaros, and others.

Polat-Demetriadou, Maria. *'Από ὅσα εἶδα καί ξέρω διά τήν 'Ελλάδα, 1940–1945* [From What I Saw and What I Know about Greece, 1940–1945] (New York, 1950) /1,5,7,R/

Poliakov, Léon and Sabille, Jacques. *Gli ebrei sotto l'occupazione Italiana* (Milan, 1956). /3/ One chapter refers to the Greek Jewry.

Porphyres, K. "'Η πνευματική ἀντίσταση μέ νόμιμα μέσα" [The Intellectual Resistance by Legal Means], *Epitheorese Technes,* 87–88 (March–April 1962), 336–365. Deals with literary and journalistic resistance "between the lines."

"Πως καί διατί οἱ Βρεταννοί ἐπρόδωσαν τήν 'Ελλάδα ἀμέσως μετά τήν κατοχήν" [How and Why the British Betrayed Greece Immediately after the Occupation], *Ethnos,* 5.–9.8.57. /1,2,4,R/

Proceedings of a Conference on Britain

and European Resistance 1939–45. Organised by St. Antony's College. (Oxford, 1962). See under Pyromaglou, Woodhouse.

Psychoundakis, George. *The Cretan Runner. His Story of the German Occupation*. Translated and introduced by P. Leigh Fermor (London: Murray, 1955). /1,2,5/ The author was runner for the leading Cretan BLOs. His pertinent reminiscences are—according to BLO Leigh Fermor—"something unique in the literature of resistance: a sort of primitive, Douanier-Rousseau war book." Indeed, the hardly literate, but literarily gifted villager provides one of the few descriptions of resistance seen "from below"—and the only in a non-Greek language.

Psyroukes, Nikos. *'Ιστορία τῆς σύγχρονης 'Ελλάδας. 1940–1967* [History of Contemporary Greece, 1940–1967]. Vol. I (Athens: Epikairoteta, 1975). /L/ Offers many (and some self-contradictory) explanations for the defeat of "the Greek anti-imperialist revolution." As main reason, however, the author offers "the counterrevolutionary and bourgeois degenerate leadership of KKE/EAM" and its lack of "ideological and organizational preparedness" for the seizure of power.

Pyromaglou, Komnenos. *'Η 'Εθνική 'Αντίστασις* [National Resistance] (Athens, 1947). 2nd enlarged ed.: 2 vols. (Athens: Dodone, 1975).

———. *'Ο Δούρειος 'Ίππος* [The Trojan Horse]. (Athens, 1958). Enlarged edition, completed by a second volume: (Athens: Dodone, 1978).

———. *'Ο Γεώργιος Καρτάλης καί ή ἐποχή του* [George Kartales and His Times]. Vol. I: 1934–1944 (Athens, 1965).

———. "La Résistance Grecque et les Alliés." In *European Resistance Movements, Second Conference*, 298–323.

———. "Servitudes d'un peuple et grandeur d'une lutte." In *Proceedings of a Conference on Britain and European Resistance* (*supra*).

———. A great number of articles in *Historike Epitheoresis* and *Historikon Archeion Ethnikes Antistaseos*, both edited by Pyromaglou himself. The author was second-in-command of EDES and turned after the war to the left (as deputy and historian). Though differing in detail, his numerous publications consistently support the central thesis of a "secret front" consisting of the Greek (royalist) Right inside and outside Greece, the British and even—at least by tacit understanding—the Germans. This heterogeneous "front" allegedly exploited the communist bogey in order to mobilize Greek anti-communists against all "democratic" (republican) resistance: EAM/ELAS, EDES and EKKA. This theory contains some elements of truth—certainly with regard to two of the supposed partners: the German occupants and their open or camouflaged Greek collaborators. But the described conspiratorial "front" never existed, as can be seen from German and British archives. (However, according to Pyromaglou, both had been partially doctored before they were opened.) Apart from analysis (which on other points is correct), Pyromaglou provides ample and valuable material on the resistance, especially on the EDES. Unfortunately, he has never defined clearly the extent of his knowledge of Zervas' "German contacts."

Ralles, Georgios I. *'Ο 'Ιωάννης Δ. Ράλλης ὁμιλεῖ ἐκ τοῦ τάφου* [Ioannes

Ralles Is Speaking from the Grave] (Athens, 1947). Apologia by the third and last occupation premier.

Regopoulos, Regas D. *Μυστικός πόλεμος. 'Ελλάδα—Μ. 'Ανατολή 1940–1945* [Secret War. Greece—Middle East 1940–1945] (Athens: Hestia, 1973). /1,4,5,R/ Interesting account on the espionage organization "5-165" led by the author. Charges the British services in the Middle East with a "leftist conspiracy" against Greek nationalist resistance.

Reid, Francis. *I Was in Noah's Ark* (London, 1957). /2,5/ Author was member of a raiding unit, working with ELAS.

Reinhardt, Gerhard. "Hellas stand auf wider die Barbaren." *Neues Deutschland,* 25.9.66. /1,2,3,6,L/

Rendel, A.M. *Appointment in Crete. The Story of a British Agent* (London, 1953) /1,2,4,5/

Rentes, Constantinos Th. *'Απολογισμός μίας 4ετίας* [Account of Four Years] (Athens, 1949). A collection of political articles.

Richter, Heinz. *Griechenland zwischen Revolution und Konterrevolution (1936–1946).* Preface by K. Pyromaglou (Frankfurt: Europäische Verlaganstalt, 1973). Greek ed. (Athens: Exantas, 1977). Originally a doctoral dissertation (Heidelberg, 1971), this is one of the most important recent works, if only for its aspiration to provide a comprehensive picture of a most critical decade in Greek history, and especially of the occupation. Unfortunately the author has failed to consult the bulk of unpublished sources available before 1971, and also to update the book edition on the basis of the British records released in the meantime. As to published material, Richter's bibliography is likewise rather inadequate, and not entirely accurate. Numerous errors in the text and in the footnotes suggest that he did not consult some of the publications cited. As a result, the author relies uncritically on the interpretations of Pyromaglou and Eudes (*supra*) and often surpasses them in doubtful and fallacious conclusions as to "British machinations," "Stalinist" (KKE's) defeatism, and the strength of idealized "democratic socialists." Generally, Richter produces a conspiratorial picture of history, cast in absolute terms of good and evil. More serious than this failure to live up to promised "objectivity" is the author's questionable use or arrangement of evidence to fit his theories. A positive exception is Richter's treatment of German occupation policy. Although based only on a small fraction of unpublished records, it is largely correct.

Roediger, Conrad. "Die internationale Hilfsaktion für die Bevölkerung Griechenlands im Zweiten Weltkrieg." *Vierteljahreshefte für Zeitgeschichte,* XI (1963), 49–71. /3,6/ Informative and balanced report on the German view of the international relief agreement to aid starving Greece.

Röhricht, Edgar. "Die Entwicklung auf dem Balkan 1943–45." *Wehrwissenschaftliche Rundschau,* XII (1962), 391–406. /3,7/

Roosevelt, Elliott. *As He Saw It.* 3rd ed. (New York, 1946). /7/ Some scattered references to events in wartime Greece.

Roth, Cecil. "The Last Days of Jewish Salonica." *Commentary,* X: 1 (July 1950), 49–55.

Roussos, Petros. *'Η μεγάλη τετραετία* [The Great Four Years]. Vol. I (n.p.: P.L.E., 1966) 2nd revised and enlarged ed. under the title: *'Η μεγάλη* πενταετία [The Great Five Years] (Athens, Synchrone Epoche, 1976/1978). /1,2,6,7,L/ Valuable source for the "orthodox" communist version of the occupation and the December 1944 events. However, the information or interpretation given is not always satisfactory, if one bears in mind that the author held a key position (permanent member and repeatedly emissary to critical conferences) in the KKE politburo throughout 1941–1944.

Sakellariou, Alexandros E. *'Η θέσις τῆς 'Ελλάδος εἰς τόν δεύτερον παγκόσμιον πόλεμον* [The Position of Greece in World War II] (New York, 1944). /4,5,R/

———. *Ένας ναύαρχος θυμᾶται ...* [An Admiral Remembers ...] (Athens, 1971). /4,5,7,R/ The author reports, in both books, his experiences as vice-premier and fleet commander during the first two years of the Greek government-in-exile. He deals in particular with the "permanent intrigues" (real or not) of his arch-enemy Tsouderos.

Saloutos, Theodoros. *The Greeks in the United States* (Cambridge, Mass., 1964). /7/ References to occupied Greece deal primarily with relief action.

Saraphes, Stephanos. *'Ο ΕΛΑΣ* [The ELAS] (Athens, 1946). The author's name is rendered as "Sarafis" in the abridged English translation: *Greek Resistance Army: The Story of ELAS* (London, 1951); the full English version: (London: Merlin Press, 1978); and in the German edition: *In den Bergen von Hellas* (East Berlin, 1964). /2,5,8,L/ The author describes his activities during the occupation, in particular after he became military commander of ELAS. Sometimes he tends to overrate his role by largely identifying the history of ELAS with his own experiences. His presentation of facts is usually correct despite frequent exaggerations concerning the military achievements of his guerrilla army. In this he obviously relied uncritically on ELAS's communiqués which were highly inflated. Furthermore, Saraphes could not avoid simplistic conclusions: in all controversial conflicts of EAM/ELAS he lays the blame on the other side (EDES, EKKA, the British, etc.). This bias should not be blamed entirely on Saraphes. As a party novice (he entered KKE secretly in the summer of 1943), the general delivered his original manuscript to the politburo for "critical reading." At the same time the text was edited in a consistent demotic language. Nevertheless, it appears that Saraphes did not allow his style and text to be fundamentally altered. Therefore, in spite of the faults and errors mentioned above, this memoir still constitutes the standard and most important primary source for ELAS and, perhaps, even for the guerrilla movement in general.

Sbarounes, Athanasios. *Μελέται καί ἀναμνήσεις ἐκ τοῦ Β΄ Παγκοσμίου Πολέμου* [Studies and Reminiscences from World War II] (Athens, 1950). /3,4,6/ Consists largely of documents and articles on the economic situation of Greece, some of them in English, French, and German.

"Σχετικά μέ τό ρόλο τοῦ Τίτο ἐνάντια στό ἑλληνικό κίνημα" [Concerning Tito's Role Against the Greek Movement], *Protoporeia* (London), 8 (Nov. 1972), 43–56. /2,7,L/ Maoist ("Marxist-Leninist") charges against the Yugoslav "agents of the Intelligence Service."

Schmidt, Walter A. *Damit Deutschland lebe* (East Berlin, 1959). /3,6,7,L/ The chapter on Greece refers to German antifascist cooperation with EAM/ELAS.

Schmidt-Richberg, Erich. *Der Endkampf auf dem Balkan* (Heidelberg, 1955). /3,6,7/ Contains a useful report on the German withdrawal from Greece by the chief of staff of "Army-group E."

Schramm-von Thadden, Ehrengard. "Der Partisanenkönig von Kreta." *Göttinger Tagblatt* 26.7.52. Impressions concerning M. Bandouvas.

———. "Nordwestgriechenland in den Kriegsjahren. Das Bevölkerungsproblem der Gebirge (1940–1949)." *Hellas* (August 1961), 27–42.

Sellenas, Spyros P. *'Η 'Ελλάς είς τόν πόλεμον* [Greece in the War] (Athens, 1946). /1,6,7/

Seth, Ronald. *The Undaunted: The Story of Resistance in Western Europe* (New York, 1956). /2,7/ Synopsis of Greek resistance containing an interesting (but not always reliable) interview with general Infante, commander of the Pinerolo division—the "first Italian unit taking sides with the Allies."

Sevastakes, Alexes. *Καπετάν Μπουκουβάλας. Τό ἀνταρτικό ἱππικό τῆς Θεσσαλίας* [Kapetan Boukouvalas. The Guerrilla Cavalry of Thessaly] (Athens: Diogenes, 1978). /2,5,L/ Based on Boukouvalas' narration to the author. Boulouvalas' [= M. Tassos] own recollections, written by himself earlier, are included in an appendix.

Siegler, Fritz Frh. von. *Die höheren Dienststellen der Deutschen Wehrmacht 1933–1945*. (München, 1953). /3,7/

Sivetides, Maximos, *'Η μάχη τῆς Κρήτης συνεχίζεται* [The Battle of Crete Goes On] (Athens: Kedros, 1979). /1,2,5,7,L/

Skandalakes, I.N. *'Αγωνίες καί τρόμοι* [Agonies and Terrors] (Athens, 1945). /2,3,5,R/ Accuses communism of "destroying the human soul," and particularly the Laconian "EAM-communist rabble" of deliberately provoking German reprisals and of murdering the patriotic population.

Sklavos, L. *'Ο ἐμφύλιος πόλεμος στήν 'Ελλάδα, 1943–49* [The Civil War in Greece, 1943–49] (n.p., n.d.). /1,2,7,L/ Trotskyite version of events, charging KKE with "bourgeois chauvinism."

Skrivanos, Nik. *Ποιός φταίει γιά τόν ἐμφύλιο πόλεμο* [Who Is to Blame for the Civil War] (Athens, 1946). /1,7,R/

Smith, Peter and Wlaker, Edwin. *War in the Aegean* (London: Kimber, 1974). Describes military operations in the Dodecanese during the autumn of 1943.

Snok, K. *'Η τραγωδία τῆς Δράμας* [The Tragedy of Drama] (Drama, 1945). /1,3,6,R/ Deals with the insurrection of autumn 1941 and with the cruel Bulgarian reprisals.

Solaro, Antonio. *Storia del Partito Communista Greco* (Milano: 1973); Greek translation, 2nd ed.: *'Ιστορία τοῦ Κομμουνιστικοῦ Κόμματος 'Ελλάδας* (Athens: Pleias, 1975). /7,L/

Soteriou, K.D. "Τό 'Εθνικό Συμβούλιο καί ἡ παιδεία" [The National Council and Education], *Epitheorese Technes,* 87–88 (March–April 1962), 300–304. /1,6,L/ Deals with education in EAM's Free Greece.

Soteropoulos, S. "'Η μάχη τῆς Κοκκινιᾶς καί τά πορίσματά της (6–9 *τοῦ Μάρτη τοῦ* 1944)" [The Battle of Kokkinia and its Lessons (March, 6–9, 1944)] *Kommounistike Epitheo-*

rese, 3 (March 1946), 142–144. /1,3,L/

Soutsos, Dem. E. *'Η 'Αθήνα στήν 'Εθνική 'Αντίσταση* [Athens in the National Resistance] (Athens, 1959). /1,R/ Provides information on some twenty nationalist resistance organizations.

Spaes, Leonidas. *Πενῆντα χρόνια στρατιώτης στήν ὑπηρεσία τοῦ ἔθνους καί τῆς δημοκρατίας* [Fifty Years Soldier in the Service of Nation and Democracy]. Vol. I (Athens, 1970). /1,5,7/

Spencer, Floyd A. *War and Postwar Greece. An Analysis Based on Greek Writings.* Washington, D.C.: Library of Congress, 1952). /1,2,3,4,7,8/ This excellent work offers a brief survey of the war and post-war period by means of bibliographical essays on the main aspects. Provides annotations for a great portion of books published before 1952.

Sporides, G. "'Ο μεγάλος διωγμός. *Τό ξεκλήρισμα τῶν 'Ελλήνων 'Εβραίων*" [The Great Persecution. The Extermination of Greek Jews], *Ethnos*, 17.1.–2.3.55.

Stadtmüller, Georg. "Haiduken und Partisanen." *Neues Abendland*, IX (1954), 267–276. /2,3,6,R/

———. "Partisanenkrieg und Völkerrecht. Südgriechenland 1943–44 als Beispiel." *Deutsches Rotes Kreuz, Schriftenreihe*, 27 (1962), 39–59. /2,3,6,R/ German historian, staff interpreter and liaison officer with the Security Battalions, describes some experiences with "nationalist" and "bolshevist" guerrillas in the Peloponnesus and questions their legal status as combatants.

Στ' Ἄρματα! Στ' Ἄρματα! Χρονικό τῆς 'Εθνικῆς 'Αντίστασης 1940–1945 [To Arms! To Arms! Chronicle of the National Resistance 1940–1945]. 4 vols. (Athens: Yannikos, 1964). /1,2,6,L/ This work, written by a committee of former EAM/ELAS members, presents the most detailed source on leftist resistance. But the "chronicle" views all intra-Greek conflicts in absolute terms and exaggerates the losses of the occupation forces.

Stathes, Constantinos E. *'Η 'Εαμική τυραννία στά Κύθηρα* [EAM's Tyranny in Kythera] (Karvounades, 1945). /1,2,5,R/

———. *Τά Κύθηρα σκλαβωμένα 1941–1946. 'Ιταλικά, γερμανικά καί ἑαμοκομμουνιστικά γεγονότα* [Enslaved Kythera, 1941–1946. Italian, German, and EAM-communist Events] (Karvounades, 1947). /1,2,3,5,7,R/

Stavrianos, L.S. *Greece. American Dilemma and Opportunity* (Chicago, 1952). /7/

———. *The Balkans Since 1453* (New York, 1958). /7/ Both books provide moderate leftist reviews of war events in Greece. The author attributes the fatal outcome of the resistance to wrong British policy (which failed to support non-communist elements inside EAM) and to KKE's unreserved "subservience to Moscow's dictates."

———. "Greece. The War and Aftermath." *Foreign Policy Reports*, XXI, 12 (1.9.45), 173–187.

———. "The Jews of Greece." *Journal of Central European Affairs*, VIII (Oct. 1948), 256–269.

———. "The Mutiny in the Greek Armed Forces (April 1944)." *American Slavic and East European Review*, IX (1950), 302–311.

———. "The Greek National Liberation Front (EAM): A Study in Resistance Organization and Administration."

Journal of Modern History, XXIV: 1 (March 1952), 42–55. In spite of its pro-EAM bias, still the best pertinent account in English.

———. and Panagopoulos, E.P. "Present-Day Greece." *Journal of Modern Greece*, XX: 2 (June 1948), 149–158. Valuable bibliographical review for 1940–47.

Stavrogiannopoulos, Vasileios. *'Η ζωή τῆς κατοχῆς καί τά τάγματα ἀσφαλείας* [Life under the Occupation and the Security Battalions] (Athens, 1966). /3,6,R/ The conclusion of this apologia: "But the Good God of Greece enlightened the then responsible men to found the Security Battalions . . ."

———. *Πικρές ἀναμνήσεις περιόδου 1941–1944* [Bitter Reminiscences from the Period 1941–1944] (Athens, 1974). /2,3,5,R/ A diary-based memoir dealing with the struggle of EDES (and of the Security Battalions) against ELAS, especially in the Nafpaktia region.

Stereff, Pantelej. "'Ορισμένες ἐκδηλώσεις τῆς ἐν ὅπλοις συναδέλφωσης τῶν 'Ελλήνων καί Βουλγάρων πατριωτῶν" [Certain Manifestations of the Fraternization in Arms Between the Greek and Bulgarian Patriots]. *Ethnike Antistase*, 9 (Dec. 1966), 935–944. French version: "La contribution du peuple grec à la lutte antifasciste de libération et certaines manifestations de la fraternité d'armes greco-bulgares." *Etudes Balkaniques*, 2–3 (1965), 37–58. The author uses unpublished Bulgarian sources.

Stering, Erich Frh von. *Jeder war ein Stück von uns.* (Neckargemünd, 1959). /2,3,5,7,R/ German officer describes his experiences of the last occupation phase in Attica and of the withdrawal from Greece. Reports cruel mutilation of captured German soldiers and collaborators by ELAS, and a probably fictitious meeting with a guerrilla leader (allegedly Markos Vaphiades).

Stockbridge, Ralph E. "Χάρις στήν 'Ελληνική 'Αντίσταση ἡττήθη ὁ Rommel" [Thanks to the Greek Resistance Rommel was Defeated], *Akropolis*, 22.–24.10.72.

Stratopoulos, Kleov. G. *'Η 'Ελληνική Βασ. Χωροφυλακή εἰς τήν ὑπηρεσίαν τῆς πατρίδος* [Greek Royal Gendarmery in the Service of the Fatherland]. 3rd ed. (Athens, 1946). /1,2,3,7,R/

Stravolemos, Dionysios Ch. *'Η Ζάκυνθος στά χρόνια τῆς σκλαβιᾶς. (1.5.41–27.3.45)* [Zante in the Years of Slavery. (1.5.41–27.3.45] (Zante, 1949). /1,3,6,R/

Sulzberger, C.L. *A Long Row of Candles. (Memoirs and Diaries 1934–1954)* (London: Macmillan, 1969). /4,5,7/

Svolos, A.I. *'Ιστορία μιᾶς προσπάθειας* [History of an Endeavor] (Athens, 1945). /1,6,7/

Sweet-Escott, Bickham. *Greece. A political and economic survey 1939–1953* (London, 1954). /7/

———. *Baker Street Irregular. (Five Years in the Special Operations Executive)* (London, 1965). /2,4,6,7/ This eye-witness report offers valuable insight into SOE history and persistent British inter-agency friction in London and the "Muddle East." Many useful references to Greece.

———. "S. O. E. in the Balkans." In Phyllis Auty and Richard Clogg, eds. *British Policy . . .*, 3–21.

Tasolambros, L. [= Lambrides, Phrixos]. *Πολιτικά σαράντα χρόνων 1909–1949* [Forty Years of Politics 1909–1949] (Athens, 1949). Discusses recent changes in the party system.

Tasoudes, Georgios N. *'Ο 'Αρχιεπίσκοπος 'Αθηνῶν Χρύσανθος* [Chrysanthos, Archbishop of Athens]. Vol. II: 1926–1949 (Athens, 1973). /1,6,7,R/ A biography by his nephew.

Tedder, Lord Arthur. *With Prejudice. The War Memoirs* (London, 1966). /7/ Information on Churchill's "passion" for the Aegean, by the Air Commander Mediterranean.

Theodorakes, Asklepios G. *'Η 'Εθνική 'Αντίστασις Κρήτης. Μέση 'Ανατολή. 1941–1945* [The National Resistance of Crete. The Middle East. 1941–1945]. 3 vols., with slightly varying titles (Herakleion, 1971/1972). /1,2,4,6,R/ Includes some rare documents.

Theologos, Nikolaos P. *'Αλέξανδρος Παπάγος* [Alexander Papagos] (Athens, 1949). /1,7,R/ "Reveals" the reasons for Papagos' imprisonment in 1943: Allegedly, Moscow had got wind of an allied project by which the general would assume command of all Greek guerrilla and Middle East forces and ordered KKE to denounce the dangerous antagonist to the Germans.

Theophanides, Phrixos. *'Ανάπηροι—οἱ πρωτοπόροι τῆς λεφτεριᾶς* [Invalids—The Pioneers of Freedom] (Athens, 1946). /1,6,L/ Deals with an EAM ancillary organization, in which most war invalids were organized.

Thesprotos, Demos. *Αὐτοκριτική. Γιατί χάθηκε ἡ λαϊκή ἐξουσία τοῦ ΕΑΜ (1940–1945)* [Autocritique. Why the People's Power of EAM Was Lost (1940–1945)] (Athens: Gutenberg, 1977). This interesting study attributes the reasons for EAM's final defeat exclusively to the faulty strategy of the KKE leadership. The author discusses other leftist interpretations and categorically rejects all (="Maoist or Trotskyite") analyses which attribute some responsibility to the USSR because of the "alleged" understanding with Great Britain.

The Struggle of the Bulgarian People against Fascism (Sofia, 1946). /1,2,3,7,L/ Contains some useful, semiofficial references to the Bulgarian role in occupied Greece.

Thomaides, G. Th. *'Ογδόντα σελίδες* [Eighty Pages] (Athens, 1947). /1,3/

Thomas, W.B. *Dare to be Free* (London, 1951). /1,3,5/ Author describes his attempts to escape from German captivity and portrays Greek solidarity as an example of spontaneous resistance in 1941.

Τό 'Απόσπασμα Βερμίου [The Vermion Detachment] (Athens, 1946). /2,6,L/

"Τό χρονικό τῆς καταστροφῆς: *'Η Κέρκυρα στίς φλόγες.*" [The Chronicle of the Catastrophy: Corfu in Flames], *Kerkyraika Nea,* Sept. 1948–11.4.49. Based on many Greek and Italian documents, this study deals with the last period prior to the German assault on the island in Sept. 1943.

Toškova, Vitka. *Bŭlgarija i Tretijat Rajch (1941–1944) Političeski otnošenija* [Bulgaria and the Third Reich (1942–1944). Political Relations] (Sofia: Nauka i izkustvo, 1975). /7,L/ Not consulted.

Toumbas, Ioannes N. *'Εχθρός ἐν ὄψει* [Enemy in Sight] (Athens, 1954). /4,5,R/ Informative report on naval activities. Biased and polemical description of political events in the Middle East.

Trechatzakes, Giangos (Kouteles). "'Εξιστόρηση διαφυγῆς κατά τήν κατοχή στήν Τουρκία" [Account of

Escape to Turkey during the Occupation], *Chiake Epitheorese,* XIII: 38/39 (1975), 69–87, 165–184.

Triantaphyllides, Costas. "Τό ἀρχεῖον τοῦ στρατηγοῦ Ζέρβα" [The Archive of General Zervas], *Apogevmatine,* 13.6.–31.10.60.

———. "1944: *'Η 'Ελλάς ὁδηγεῖται εἰς τήν τραγωδίαν τοῦ Δεκεμβρίου*" [1944. Greece is Led twoards the Tragedy of December], *Apogevmatine,* 2.11.64–2.1.65. Author had previously compiled and edited Zervas' memoirs (*infra*). Both series of articles also rely on the general's archives and provide much old and some new material, especially on EDES. To be used with caution with respect to other organizations or wider conclusions.

———. "Ντοκουμέντα & *μαρτυρίες ἀπό τά χρόνια τῆς φωτιᾶς.* (1942–1945) *'Η ὑπόθεση τοῦ γιατροῦ Καρακατσάνη.*" [Documents and Depositions from the Years of the Fire, (1942–1945). The Case of Dr. Karakatsanes] *Kathemerine* 9.5.76–21.10.76. The intricate story of alleged German agent and his frightful end.

Triarius. *Septembre '43. La tragedie de la Cefalonia* (Rome, 1945).

Tsakalotos, Thrasyvoulos I. *40 χρόνια στρατιώτης τῆς 'Ελλάδος* [40 Years Soldier of Greece]. Vol. I (Athens, 1960). /1,4,5,7,R/

———. *'Η μάχη τῶν ὀλίγων* [The Battle of the Few] (Athens, 1971). /1,4,6,7,R/

Tsatsos, Th. D. *Αἱ παραμοναί τῆς ἀπελευθερώσεως* [The Eve of Liberation] (Athens, 1950). 2nd ed. Introduced and commented by Pan. Kanellopoulos (Athens: Ikaros, 1973). /4,5/ Usually reliable account as to the facts, but somewhat exaggerated in its conclusions owing to its apologetic character. The author voices unreserved approval of Papandreou's policy, whereas he blames "Venizelist" (liberal) opposition, thereby defending his own defection from the Liberals to the premier's party. Yet this remains one of the most informative sources on the period between the Lebanon Conference and the liberation of Greece (especially the 2nd ed.) enriched by Kanellopoulos' comments and numerous diary excerpts qualifying Tsatsos' animosity against the Liberals.

Tsatsou, Ioanna. *Φύλλα κατοχῆς* [Occupation Pages] (Athens, 1965). English ed.: Tsatsos, Jeanne. *The Sword's Fierce Edge* (Nashville: Vanderbilt University Press, 1969). /1,3,5/ Good account, contains information on EKKA and Archbishop Damaskenos' work.

Tsellos, E. K. *'Η συμβολή τῆς 'Ελλάδος στή συμμαχική νίκη* [The Contribution of Greece to the Allied Victory] (Athens, 1946). /7/

Tsigantes, Chr. "'Η Μέση 'Ανατολή" [The Middle East], *Ethnos,* 14.2.–30.4.55. /4,5/

———. "'Ο 'Ιερός Λόχος" [The Sacred Battalion], *Ethnos,* 2.5.–20.8.55. /1,4,6/

Tsirimokos, Elias. *'Αντιφασιστικά* [Antifascist Writings]. 2nd ed. (Athens, 1946). /L/ Collection of pre-war publications. The prologue (pp. iii–xxviii) discusses these views in the light of antifascist experiences, 1941–44.

———. *'Αλέξανδρος Σβῶλος. 'Η δική μας ἀλήθεια* [Alexander Svolos. Our Truth] (Athens, 1962). /1,6/

———. "Συνοδοιπόροι" [Fellow-travellers], *Mache,* 5.9.–19.12.48. /1,2,6/

———. "Τοῦ ὕψους καί τοῦ βάθους" [Ups and Downs], *Anexartetos Typos,* 4.7.–17.8.60.

———. "Τά ἀπομνημονεύματα" [The Memoirs], *Akropolis,* 21.1.–24.3.73. Author describes with skill and interest his experiences as prominent "fellow-traveller" of KKE in EAM. But, remarkably, all series are largely identical, not only in substance but even in wording—without any reference to the previous ones. Only the "memoirs" contain some new documents and (authentic?) diary excerpts.

Tsirkas, Strates. "'Η πνευματική ἀντίσταση στή Μέση 'Ανατολή" [Intellectual Resistance in the Middle East], *Epitheorese Technes,* 87–88 (March–April 1962), 480–501. /4,6,L/ Very informative review.

Tsolakoglou, Georgios K. *'Απομνημονεύματα* [Memoirs] (Athens, 1959). /3,5,7/ Account of the first occupation premier. Seems to be written largely in good faith, in spite of some errors and fallacious conclusions.

Tsoucalas, Constantine. *The Greek Tragedy* (Harmondsworth: Penguin, 1969). /7/ Contains a useful survey of occupation events.

Tsouderos, E.I. *'Ελληνικές ἀνωμαλίες στή Μέση 'Ανατολή* [Greek Anomalies in the Middle East] (Athens, 1945). /4,6,8/

———. *'Ο ἐπισιτισμός* [Provisioning] (Athens, 1946).

———. *Γνώμες καί λόγοι* [Opinions and Speeches] (Athens, 1946).

———. *'Επισιτισμός 1941–44. Μέση 'Ανατολή* [Provisioning 1941–44. The Middle East] (Athens, 1948).

———. *Διπλωματικά παρασκήνια 1941–1944* [Behind the Diplomatic Scenes 1941–1944] (Athens, 1950). In his various pertinent publications, the head of the 1941–44 Government-in-exile tries hard for a multiple apologia. In his two books on provisioning, he attempts to reject all charges of having disregarded starving Greece; in the others (especially 1945), he portrays himself as an undaunted Cassandra, who pointed out the imminent danger of "anomalies," but who was ignored by George II and his British patrons. In reality, Tsouderos never dared to force (even by threat of resignation) the King to commit himself not to return prior to a plebiscite. And during the resistance mission to Cairo (summer 1943), it was primarily the premier's attitude which once again enabled George II (and Churchill) to avoid any commitment. Nevertheless, another sad postwar myth cultivated by Tsouderos involves the dilemma of a democratic premier serving an authoritarian king by patriotic duty. In 1945, he even put monarchism on a par with communism, seeing both as "the same violent and dictatorial reaction," whereas in his unpublished diary (e.g., 1942) he had identified his own with the King's conception of democracy which "doesn't lose its essence by the restriction of parliamentary deviations." Despite (and perhaps even because of) these foibles, Tsouderos' reminiscences are still indispensable for the history of the Greek government-in-exile.

Tzimas, Andreas. "'Ο Στ. Σαράφης στό ἀρχηγεῖο τοῦ ΕΛΑΣ" [Stephanos Saraphes in the ELAS headquarters], *Eleftbere Hellada* (Rome), 10.12.70–11.2.71. (Reproduction of *Pyrsos,* Dresden, 1 and 6 (1967). /2,5,L/ The political adviser of ELAS provides extremely valuable material on Saraphes' volte-face, and generally on the development of ELAS and its relations with the British during the decisive spring of 1943.

Ufficio Storico della Marina Militare, ed.

La Marina Italiana nella seconda guerra mondiale. Vol. XVI/2: *Attività dopo l'armistizio—Avvenimenti in Egeo*. (Rome, 1957). Detailed information about the events in the Eastern Aegean (Sept.–Oct. 1943) and the "heroic" Italian defense against the former German ally.

Vades G. "Τά γεγονότα στίς ἑλληνικές ἔνοπλες δυνάμεις τῆς Μέσης 'Ανατολῆς" [The Events Involving the Greek Troops of the Middle East], *Elefthere Hellada* (Rome), 4.7.74. /4,L/

Valaoras, V.G. "Some Effects of Famine on the Population of Greece." *The Milbank Memorial Fund Quarterly,* XXIV (1946), 215–234.

Valetas, G. "Οἱ διανοούμενοι στόν 'Αγώνα" [The Intellectuals in the Struggle], *Aiolika Grammata,* V: 29 (1975), 345–357. First issued as a brochure by the Athenian EAM in Sept. 1945.

———. "Σελίδες ἀπό τήν ἱστορία τῆς ἐθνικῆς Λεσβιακῆς ἀντίστασης" [Pages from the History of the National Resistance in Lesbos], *Aiolika Grammata,* V: 29(1975), 387–402. /1,8,7,L/

Valioules, Stergios. *Πολίτης Β΄ κατηγορίας* [Second-Class Citizen] (Athens: Gutenberg, 1975). /1,2,5,L/ Deals with resistance in Eastern Macedonia.

Verdes, Pyrros *Οἱ κλοῦβες.* [The Cages] (Athens, 1946). /1,2,5,L/ Describes the life of hostages in concentration camps and in special iron-cage vehicles (klouves) until their liberation by ELAS.

Vassilas, E. "Τέσσαρες μῆνες μέ τόν ΕΛΑΣ" [Four Months with ELAS], *Eleftheria,* 27.2.–12.3.55. /2,5/ Report by a general who left ELAS because of the communist dominance within it.

Vazaios, Emmanouel. *Τά ἄγνωστα παρασκήνια τῆς 'Εθνικῆς 'Αντιστάσεως εἰς τήν Πελοπόννησον* [The Unknown Behind-the-Scenes Events of the National Resistance in the Peloponnesus] (Corinth, 1961). /2,5/ Interesting account by an officer who started in a nationalist guerrilla organization, was then captured by ELAS, and finally converted.

Venezes, Elias. *'Αρχιεπίσκοπος Δαμασκηνός. Οἱ χρόνοι τῆς δουλείας* [Archbishop Damaskenos. The Years of Slavery] (Athens, 1962). /1,3/

———. *'Εμμανουήλ Τσουδερός* [Emmanuel Tsouderos] (Athens, 1966). /4,7/

———. "῞Οταν λάμπει ἡ ὀρθοδοξία: *'Αρχιεπίσκοπος Δαμασκηνός, ἀρχηγός τῆς 'Εκκλησίας, ὅταν τό ἔθνος ἐχειμάζετο στούς χρόνους τῆς κατοχῆς*" [When Orthodoxy Glows: Archbishop Damaskinos, Chief of the Church when the Nation Was Ravaged during the Occupation Years], *Mesemvrine,* 7.–10.2.62 These biographies are well-written and contain plenty of material on the respective scenes of action (occupied Athens, the Middle East), but are uncritical about the principal character.

Venizelos, Sophokles E. "'Από τό ἡμερολόγιόν μου διά τά ἐν Μέση 'Ανατολῆ" [From My Diary about the Events in the Middle East], *Hellenike Hemera,* 6.12.51–24.1.52. /4,5/ Valuable account by the former minister, vice-premier, and eventually premier, somewhat marred by the author's attempt to appear generally more resolute than in reality he was, and more stern towards leftist mutineers, British officials, etc.

Veopoulos, S. *Τό σφάλμα* [The Fault]. Vol. I (Athens, 1961). Interesting essays on persons, parties, and aspects of the resistance.

Vlachos, Speros. *'Απομνημονεύματα.* [Memoirs]. Vol II (Athens: Nousias, 1975). /2,5,7/ Provides first-hand information on the 5/42 Evzone Regiment of EKKA and the post-war quarrels among the surviving cadres.

Vlantas, Demetres. *'Η προδομένη έπανάσταση 1941–44. Πολιτική 'Ιστορία KKE* [The Betrayed Revolution 1941–44. Political History of the KKE] (Athens: Evangeliou, 1977). /1,2,6/ Prominent ex-communist denounces his former comrades in the party leadership. In spite of much useful information, this account is to be used with caution.

Vlontakes, Stavros G. *'Η "'Οχυρά Θέσις Κρήτης".* ["Stronghold Crete"] (Athens, 1975). /1,2,6,L/ Deals with the strange situation in the region of Chania where a German evacuation could not be realized in September 1944, and therefore the occupation continued until the summer of 1945.

Vogel, Georg. *Diplomat unter Hitler und Adenauer* (Düsseldorf: Econ, 1969). /3,5,7/ German diplomat in Athens reports on German inter-service difficulties and on the embassy's impotence to intervene on a large scale in the activities of other authorities, such as reprisals, deportation of Jews, etc.

Voigt, F.A. "Greece, the Empire and the United States," *The Nineteenth Century and After,* CXLI (1947), 186–190, 221–231, 287–294. /R/

———. *Pax Britannica* (London, 1949). /1,2,7,R/ Chapter V deals with the "Greek War of Independence" and its political aspects. Accuses ELAS of collaboration and states that royalists "probably had more supporters in Greece than any other party."

Volterakes, Antonios. *Εἰς τήν ὑπηρεσίαν τῆς Γκεστάπο* [In Gestapo's Service] (Athens, 1946). /1,3,6/

[Voudoures, Panos]. *'Υπό τό φῶς τῆς ἀλήθειας. Αἱ ὀργανώσεις ἀντιστάσεως Βορείου 'Ελλάδος* [Under the Light of Truth. The Resistance Organizations of Nothern Greece] (Thessaloniki, 1948). /1,2,6,R/

Voulgarakes, Damianos A. *Σφαγή στό Δομένικο* [Slaughter in Domenico] (Larissa, 1963). /1,3/

Voulgares, Stergios. *'Ο Γοργοπόταμος* [The Gorgopotamos] (Athens, 1971). /2,5,R/ Provides the (radical) EDES version of the Gorgopotamos operation. The preface by Metropolitan Serapheim of Yannina is likewise strongly hostile against EAM.

Vukmanović, Svetozar (Tempo). "Kommunistička Partija Grčke i narodnooslobodilačka borba" [The KKE in the People's Liberation Struggle], *Borba,* 29.8.–1.9.49. /2,6,L/

———. *Über die Volksrevolution in Griechenland* (Belgrade, 1950). English ed.: *How and Why the People's Liberation Struggle of Greece Met with Defeat* (London, 1950). The instalments in *Borba* and particularly the enlarged (and somewhat modified) book edition represent the official Yugoslav response (translated in many languages) to accusations by the Greek comrades (*La trahison . . . , supra*). The author was Tito's confidant and political emissary for Macedonia; he charges the KKE with anti-leninism, chauvinism, and "cruel oppression of the Macedonian people," a "rotten defeatist" strategy towards British imperialism and much more.

———. *The Ongoing Revolution* (London: Macdonald, 1972). /5,7,L/ Some references to the author's conflicts with KKE leaders and BLOs. Charges ELAS with passivity.

———. "Ο Τέμπο γιά τήν 'Ελληνική 'Αντίσταση" [Tempo on Greek Resistance] *Elefthere Hellada,* Rome, 9.3.72.

———. "Νά γιατί ἔχασε ὁ ΕΛΑΣ τόν πόλεμο" [Here is Why ELAS Lost the War], *Ta Nea,* 19.–20.1.76. Two interviews in which Tempo again—but more politely—criticizes the war leadership of the KKE and of ELAS (except Ares).

Wilson, Henry M. *Eight Years Overseas, 1939–1947* (London, 1951). /2,4,5,7/ Author was Army Commander Middle East, later Mediterranean, and provides—despite some gross mistakes—an informative high-level account of British inter-agency friction, much of it due to quarrels about the "guidance" of Greek resistance.

Woodhouse, C.M. *Apple of Discord* (London, 1948). Greek ed.: (Athens: Exantas, 1976). /1,2,3,4,6,8/

———. *The Struggle for Greece, 1941–1949* (London: Hart-Davis/MacGibbon, 1976). /1,2,6,7/

———. "Prolegomena to a Study of Resistance," *The Nineteenth Century and After,* CLXIV (1948), 269–276; CLXV (1949), 86–93.

———. Letter in *Eleftheria,* 17.3.55.

———. "Zur Geschichte der Resistance in Griechenland," *Vierteljahreshefte für Zeitgeschichte,* VI: 2 (1958), 138–150.

———. "The Greek Resistance, 1942–44." In *European Resistance Movements, First Conference,* (*supra*), 374–390.

———. "Britain and Greece." In *Proceedings . . .* (*supra*).

———. "'Η 'Ελληνική 'Εθνική 'Αντίστασις ὅπως τήν ἔζησα μέ τούς ἀντάρτες τοῦ ΕΔΕΣ καί τοῦ ΕΑΜ-ΕΛΑΣ" [The Greek National Resistance as I Witnessed It with the Guerrillas of EDES and EAM-ELAS], *Akropolis,* 11.4.–9.6.65.

———. "Early British Contacts with the Greek Resistance in 1942," *Balkan Studies,* XXII: 2 (1971), 347–363.

———. "The 'Revolution' in its Historical Context." In R. Clogg and G. Yannopoulos, eds. *Greece under Military Rule* (London, 1972), 1–16.

———. "Summer 1943: The Critical Months." In Phyllis Auty and Richard Clogg, eds. *British Policy . . . ,* 117–146. The author was deputy commander then commander of the British (later, Allied) Military Mission (AMM) with the Greek guerrillas. Most of his accounts are less autobiographical than analytical studies on the political aspects of the occupation and the resistance. He underrates the military significance of guerrilla warfare, thereby deepening the differences that separate his work from the bulk of the pertinent Greek literature. Regarding his political conclusions, the reader must be cautious not to be swept along by the author's excellent style and the sagacious argumentation. In his explanation of the British role, bias is inevitable, and Woodhouse admits that he seeks to justify British policy as "the only possible" one. He especially wants to demonstrate that but for AMM "the Communists would have been in total control of Greece" in the autumn of 1944 (*Apple of Discord*). At any rate, British records contain ample material proving that Woodhouse was not the Machiavellian "Satan of English imperialism," as he is characterized in pro-EAM works (e.g., Chatzepanagiotou), and that he sincerely strove to avoid guerrilla civil war. His failure convinced him even more that EAM-ELAS was "both the creation and creature" of a rather sinister KKE, and accordingly he inclined towards its antagonists—especially Zervas' EDES. For nearly three decades, Woodhouse denied all collaboration charges against the latter, to be finally convinced by German documentary evidence (preface to the Greek edition of *Apple of Discord;* also *The Struggle for Greece*). The author is misinformed on some other specific points (e.g., of the "communist sphere") and his dating of events is often imprecise. A few flagrant mistakes in *The Struggle for Greece* are due to reliance on unreliable sources, avoided in most of his earlier publications. Among his articles, the one in *Akropolis* is the most autobiographical and also the most anti-EAM account. The article in *Balkan Studies* provides valuable SOE material not covered elsewhere. To sum up, despite these reservations, and even after the opening of British (political) records, C.M. Woodhouse's works are still indispensable for every student of Greek resistance.

Woodward, Sir Llewellyn. *British Foreign Policy in the Second World War.* Vol. III, 2nd enlarged ed. (London: HMSO, 1971). /2,4,7,8/ Author presents, in chapter XLIII, the official British position on "policy towards Greece, April 1941–August 1945." Based on Foreign Office records.

Xeradake, Koula. *Κατοχικά. Κατάλογοι ἐκτελεσθέντων—φωτογραφίες—ντοκουμέντα—ἐνθύμια ἀπό τόν ἐθνικό ἀπελευθερωτικό ἀγώνα 1941–44* [Occupation Events. Catalogs of Executed—Photographs—Documents—Mementos from the National Liberation Struggle 1941–44]. 2 vols. (Athens, 1975/1979). /1,3,L/

Xydis, Stephen G. *Greece and the Great Powers, 1944–1947* (Thessaloniki, 1963). The introductory chapters contain useful background information on the occupation period.

———. "The Secret Anglo-Soviet Agreement on the Balkans of October 9, 1944, *Journal of Central European Affairs,* XV (Oct. 1955), 248–271.

Zachariades, Nikos. *Ἡ Ἑλλάδα στό δρόμο τοῦ λαϊκοῦ δημοκρατικοῦ μετασχηματισμοῦ* [Greece on the Way to Popular Democratic Transformation] (New York, 1945). /7,L/

———. *Καινούργια κατάσταση—καινούργια καθήκοντα* [New Situation—New Duties] (Nicosia, 1950).

———. *Τά προβλήματα καθοδήγησης στό ΚΚΕ* [The Problems of Guidance in the KKE] (n.p., 1952). The KKE leader repeatedly discusses communist strategy in the resistance. However, in his 1945 work Zachariades still endorses the "absolutely correct basic line" of his substitutes: "EAM, from the beginning until the end of the Occupation, fundamentally was on the right track." And only after Siantos' death is he accused by Zachariades as a "dirty traitor" imposing on EAM a chauvinist and defeatist policy, etc.

Zalakostas, Chrestos. *Τό χρονικό τῆς σκλαβιᾶς* [The Chronicle of Slavery] (Athens, n.d.). /1,2,5,8,R/ This first-hand account by a prominent member of Athenian nationalist resistance repeatedly vilifies Greek (republican and especially communist) rivals. Yet this interesting memoir is worth reading and should be consulted for any resistance history of occupied Athens.

Zanantris [=Adrianopoulou, Ioanna]. *Ἐθνική δρᾶσις καί ἀντίδρασις.*

Πόλεμος-Κατοχή [National Action and Reaction. War-Occupation] (Athens, 1947)./1,3,5,7,R/ Describes the author's resistance efforts by means of benefit performances in her semi-real world of stage and poetry. Differentiation between 'patriotic' and "traitorous" members of the collaborationist administration is certainly influenced by her personal sympathies and experiences.

Zannas, A. *Κατοχή* [Occupation]. (Athens, 1964). /1,5/

Zapheiropoulos, Dem. G. *Τό KKE καί ή Μακεδονία* [The KKE and Macedonia] (Athens, 1948). /2,7,R/

Zecev, Marian. "*La résistance et la guerre civile—thème fructueux pour la nouvelle littérature grecque. Études Balkaniques,* XI: 3 (1975), 11–29.

Zentner, Kurt, ed. *Illustrierte Geschichte des Widerstandes in Deutschland und Europa, 1933–1945* (München: Südwest, 1966). /1,2,7/

Zepos, Demetrios. *Λαϊκή δικαιοσύνη είς τάς ἐλευθέρας περιοχάς τῆς ὑπό κατοχήν 'Ελλάδος* [People's Justice in the Free Areas of Occupied Greece] (Athens, 1945). /1,2,8/ This impartial description of the "people's courts" set up by EAM is still an essential source in spite of some gaps and errors.

Zerbas, Dionysios D. *Σημειώσεις ἀπό τήν κατοχή τῶν Παξῶν ὑπό τῶν 'Ιταλῶν (21.5.1941–2.10.1943) καί τῶν Γερμανῶν (2.10.43–15.7.1944)* [Notes from the Occupation of Paxoi by the Italians (21.5.1941–2.10.1943) and by the Germans (2.10.1943–15.7.1944)] (Athens, 1973). /R/

Zervas, Napoleon. "Ἔκθεσις, 22.6.49" [Report, 22.6.49], *Historike Epitheorese, 8–9 (1965), 322–338.* Synoptic account on EDES, 1941–1945.

———. "Τά ἀπόρρητα ἔγραφά μου" [My Secret Documents], *Akropolis, 13.11.49–27.5.50.*

———. "Τά ἄγνωστα παρασκήνια τῆς ἀντιστάσεως, *τοῦ ἐμφυλίου πολέμου καί τῆς συμμαχικῆς πολιτικῆς εἰς τήν 'Ελλάδα κατά τό διάστημα τῆς κατοχῆς*" [The Unknown Behind-the-Scenes Events of the Resistance, the Civil War, and of Allied Policy in Occupied Greece], *Apogevmatine,* 29.7.–10.12.57. These controversial accounts by the EDES leader are indispensable for a balanced history of guerrilla warfare and serve—despite their extreme bias—as a counterweight to partisan accounts by the other side. (See also under Triantaphyllides.)

Zevgos, Yiannes. "ΠΕΕΑ, *ή πρώτη λαϊκοδημοκρατική κυβέρνηση*" [PEEA, the First People's Democratic Government], *Kommounistike Epitheorese,* 4 (April 1946), 160–163.

Zographos, Alekos. *'Ο Ἄρης Βελουχιώτης καί ή ἀλήθεια γιά τό Γοργοπόταμο* [Ares Velouchiotes and the Truth about Gorgopotamos] (Athens, 1962); 2nd enlarged ed. (Athens: Askraios, 1975). /2,6,L/

Zographos, Zissis. "Über den nationalen Kampf des griechischen Volkes." In Kommission . . . , IV, 267–272. /1,2,L/

———. "Δόξα στήν ἀντίσταση" [Glory to the Resistance], *Avge,* 15.–18.10.64.

Zoides, G., et al. *'Ιστορία τῆς 'Εθνικῆς 'Αντίστασης 1940–1945* [History of National Resistance 1940–1945] (Athens: Nea Vivlia, 1974). /L/ Somewhat panegyrical work; attributes defeat of EAM and KKE not to their faults, but almost exclusively to the "satanic" British intrigues.

Zotiades, George B. *The Macedonian Controversy* (Thessaloniki, 1954). /7/

Zotos, Stephanos. *Greece. The Struggle for Freedom* (New York, 1967). /1,2,4,7/

Part Two

Jews in Wartime Greece

A Select Annotated Bibliography

Steven Bowman

Introduction

The policy of the Nazi government to seek out Jews and other minority groups for extermination is unprecedented and hence difficult for historians to comprehend and analyze. True, innocent people were killed indiscriminately during the war: in Greece whole villages were liquidated as part of the German policy of reprisal and punishment. Still, none of these victims were singled out for death a priori, simply because of their ethnic or religious origin.

At the same time one must not restrict the story of the Jews during the war years to the tragedy of their collective death. To do so would deny to one element of the Greek body politic the recognition it deserves for its civic and military participation in the Greek-Italian campaigns of 1940–1941 and its contributions to the resistance.

With the withdrawal of the German army from Greece, a new set of problems confront the historian of the period. The few thousand Jews who came back from the mountains and the occasional stragglers from the death camps who returned to claim their homes and property arrived in the midst of the civil war that was then breaking out. The hostile reception they encountered caused a number of these Jews to emigrate to Israel or the United States. The attitude of the various post-war governments toward the Jewish property claims has formed an interesting and continuing chapter in contemporary Greek politics.

The virtual absence of Jews in post-war Greece necessitates a special note. Since Jews had been prominent in the intellectual, cultural, social, and economic life of pre-war Greece, the destruction of their communities during the war created a vacuum in the corresponding industrial and social infrastructures during the period of rebuilding at the end of the 1940s and the subsequent decade. A prosopographic analysis of the post-war economy would show a corresponding shift in the economic pursuits of the new Greek society. The study of modern Greece therefore should not exclude one basic cause for these shifts, namely, the virtual elimination of one specialized segment of the nation's population and its consequences.

Today a decimated Jewish community (perhaps 5,000 of a pre-war population of approximately 80,000) enjoys the privileges of citizenship in Greek society. These Jews are heir to a 2,500-year-old diaspora that has

The author thanks the Memorial Foundation for Jewish Culture for its continued support of his research in Greek-Jewish history. A general survey of the Jewish experience in Greece can be found in the author's forthcoming survey "Jews in Wartime Greece."

been marked by a number of specialized vicissitudes over the millennia. The major outline of their story has been recorded by scholars over the past three generations; however, it has yet to be incorporated into the mainstream of general Greek history. Nor is the story of the Jews in Greece during the tragic decade of the 1940s well-known to the general public. The scholarly world too has generally ignored the implications of their experiences for the particular, no less than the general, history of the period. This is not the place to comment on the contemporary attempts by purported scholars and various nationalist propagandists and apologists to deny or otherwise obscure the extent of the destruction of the Jewish communities throughout Europe.

The following bibliography is not to be considered exhaustive; undoubtably there are other articles and ephemera (see Friedman, 1953 in Section II) to be found in the myriad of languages that constitute the source material for the study of the war years. The present list therefore should be considered as an introduction that will provide the student and scholar with a guide to the major manuscript and printed sources available on the subject. Section I also includes summaries of a few of the memoirs to be found in Jerusalem. These have been chosen to illustrate a valuable but untapped resource for the history of the resistance and life in free Greece in general.

The bibliography lists manuscript sources in various archives. Very few of these can be considered official documents since, aside from Jewish organizations, few governments were interested in this aspect of the Jewish problem during the war. Rather, their concern was with those Jews who could claim a foreign citizenship, namely Spanish, Turkish, Italian, American, British, and so forth. The American archives also represent a sad sequence of telegrams from the U.S. consulate in Istanbul to the Department of State in Washington describing the memoirs of the refugees, while the official story is concerned with the attempt of Great Britain to stem any flow of refugees toward Palestine.

In addition to memoirs on tape, in manuscript, and in print, a number of observations by skilled reporters and scholars have been included in Section II. Some of the remarks by Greek-Jewish journalists and professionals have been called into question. Claims have been made that these are self-serving or contain false information. All this is to be expected in the recording of such traumatic experiences. However, the more material that is made available, the better historians of future generations will be able to perform their task. Since many of the participants in the wartime story are still alive, their memoirs should be recorded for posterity, despite their understandable reticence to reopen old wounds. With respect to research into the Jewish aspect of the problem, such sources must be assiduously cultivated since there is precious little official documentation on the subject.

I. Unpublished Memoirs and Archival Materials

1. United States:
   The Center for Holocaust Studies
   1609 Avenue J
   Brooklyn, N.Y. 11230

Dr. Michael Matsas has kindly donated a copy of his unpublished manuscript, "The Illusion of Safety," and all of his research material (Reference: Greek Jews—Matsas) to the Center for Holocaust Studies. This valuable collection includes:

a) Thirteen wartime reports from the British Public Record Office (FO 371 37210 06179 summarizes the efforts of the Skouras brothers of Hollywood in Greek War-Relief Activity).
b) Declassified material from the United States National Archives containing dispatches from May 11, 1943 to May 7, 1944.
c) Several files from the Jewish Agency for Palestine.
d) Xerox copies of wartime newspapers and other ephemera.
e) Yad VaShem (see below) files verifying efforts of Greek Christians who assisted Jews.
f) A number of Yad VaShem interviews (see below), some with an appended English translation.
g) An exchange of letters with the widow and son of Rabbi Zvi Koretz and a translation of her memoir deposited in Jerusalem.
h) Several dozen letters in Greek from Jewish participants in the resistance and other wartime survivors.

2. Israel: Central Archives for the History of the Jewish People, Hebrew University of Jerusalem. Communal and private archives and correspondence dating from ca. 1890 through the 1940s from the communities of Athens, Kavalla, Komotini, Rhodes, Thessaloniki, Volos, Xanthi, and Yannina.

3. Israel: The Institute for Contemporary Jewry, Oral History Division, Hebrew University of Jerusalem. Approximately twenty-five interviews with Greek Jews in Greek, English, and Hebrew covering the 1930s and 1940s.

4. Israel: Yad VaShem, Martyrs' and Heroes' Remembrance Authority, Jerusalem. Over fifty interviews, mostly in Hebrew, dealing with the 1940s; also a number of German documents and memoirs including the transcripts of the Eichmann trial and files documenting the roles of the Righteous Gentiles.

5. Several of the Yad VaShem memoirs and interviews are of immediate interest and of value for the light they shed on aspects of the resistance in Greece. A summary of a few will indicate their value for researchers:

#03/2989. Records an escape from Bulgarian persecutions in Kavalla. Interviewee reached Athens in September 1942 and enrolled in the university where he studied economics; description of that terrible winter with observations on the functioning of the black market. General Organization of Agricultural Institutes in Greece received permission from Germans to regulate trade in kind: fifty to sixty chapters were established. Within this framework weapons and printed matter freely circulated. Interviewee in charge of fifty-two villages in area of Elassona; organized farmers' co-operative by emphasizing that it was against the black market and not political, i.e., he had nothing to do with the attempt of EAM to establish its political/economic organization in the area. Still, EAM controlled the overall organization, but he dealt only with ELAS representatives for whom he organized food and cover. Interviewee expressed a desire to join fighters but was convinced that he was more valuable in carrying out liaison and logistics work. The important fact about this organization was its legality: it was recognized by the Germans. Also it involved the villagers in mutual economic cooperation. At the end of the war, despite invitations by villagers to remain and continue his work, interviewee left Elassona to seek out his family. Only his sister survived; she had been taken by ELAS to the hills surrounding Volos.

#03/2990. Contains story of a Jew from Kavalla who joined ELAS on Mount Olympos. His task was to accompany Germans as an interpreter on their rounds through the mountain villages when they "purchased" food and supplies.

#03/2688. Report of a Jew from Thessaloniki who joined ELAS on Mount Olympos. His task was to act as liaison with British bombers who dropped weapons and gold coins in packets of fifty kilograms. Later he was placed in charge of the weapons dropped: he was aided in his activity by 630 Italian prisoners held by ELAS. After participating in the liberation of Lamia ("40,000 partisans converged on Lamia"), he began to send his Italian charges home. After the Varkiza agreement Jews laid down their arms or surrendered them to the British and returned to their former homes. Jews refused to participate in any civil war between Greeks; their fight was against the Italian, Bulgarian, and German invaders of Greece.

#03/2487. Interviewee was drafted first in Thessaloniki, becoming secretary to the leader of the guerrilla band because of his knowledge of Greek, i.e., actually became tutor to the leader's two sons. One day he heard that communists were coming to attack royalists and refused to participate in a battle between Greeks. After the communists' victory he was captured, and eventually communists learned that he was a Jew. He was given a typewriter and told to translate French and Italian documents into Greek; received officer grade and worked in office of SO EAM/ELAS. The Quartermaster was a Jew from Thessaloniki.

#03/2484. The report of Isaac Cohen, an eyewitness to the Sonderkommando revolt from the vantage point of the Kanadakommando. Since he spoke Greek, Spanish, French, some German and Polish (which he learned in the camp), he was the outside liaison with the Greeks in the Sonderkommando. The Greek Jews in Crematorium #3 died singing partisan songs as well as the traditional songs the Greeks used to sing when the Turks herded the Christians into the churches to be burnt alive.

#03/2491. The interviewee joined the

Greek army in 1939 and later fought in Albania. After demobilization he returned to Thessaloniki, later fled to Larissa to escape arrest, then to Athens and finally to safety in Çesme via the Euboean escape route. He joined the Greek army in the Middle East but during rest and recuperation in Gaza he deserted and went to Tel Aviv in 1943.

#03/2703. A lengthy interview with a Yemenite Jew from Palestine who was captured by the Germans in Kalamata. He escaped and hid with a Greek family near Larissa. There he memorized parts of the New Testament in Greek and passed himself off as a protestant from Jerusalem. At time of interview he still spoke some Greek that the family had taught him.

#03/2485. The report of a Jewess from Thessaloniki who was sent to Auschwitz. She relates how the young Greek-Jewish girls (i.e., those who had not been selected for extermination) used to sing the melancholy tunes of Greek tradition. The German guards used to gather round their barracks to listen.

#03/2793. Contains the unpublished memoir of Dr. Marco Nahon from Didymotikon entitled "Birkenau. The Camp of Death" (translated from French by Jacqueline Havaux, copyright, 1959). It compares with the published memoir of Dr. Albert Menasche (see Part II).

6. Michael N. Matsas, "The Illusion of Safety," unpublished manuscript that contains personal reminiscences of destruction and resistance, as well as newly declassified documents (see above #1).

Dr. Rae Dalven is completing two manuscripts: a play dealing with the Jews in Athens during the war years and the story of the Jews in her native Yannina. Chapters of the latter have appeared in *The Sephardic Scholar* and elsewhere. The Institute for Research of Thessaloniki Jewry in Tel Aviv has a manuscript (in French) by a member of the Sonderkommando who survived the revolt. The author avers the role of the Greek Jews in the revolt and lists another eleven Greek survivors.

II. Published Memoirs and Secondary Studies

Ainsztein, Reuben. *Jewish Resistance in Nazi-Occupied Eastern Europe* (London, 1974). Pages 769ff contain a long and detailed account of the revolt in Auschwitz, but do not include any discussion of the role and participation of any particular group of Jews. Author does not cite any of the Greek memoirs on the subject.

Ali, Henrietta. "Thanks to the Passport. A Report of a Survivor from Salonica on the Way from Bergen-Belson to Palestine," *Reshumoth,* n.s., Vol. II (Tel Aviv, 1945–46), pp. 41–43 (in Hebrew).

Arditi, Benjamin. *Yehudei Bulgariah bishnot ha-mishpat ha-nazi: 1940–1944* [The Jews of Bulgaria during the Years of the Nazi Occupation: 1940–1944] (Tel Aviv, 1962) (in Hebrew). Cites a number of Bulgarian documents in his treatment of the Jews in Thrace and Macedonia.

———. "El heroe Dr. Saul Mezan," *Ozar Yehudei Sepharad* (= Tesoro de los Judios Sefardies), IV (1961), pp. 168–69 (in Hebrew). On the wartime fate of this Bulgarian journalist in Thessaloniki and Yannina.

Avni, Haim. "Spanish Nationals in Greece and Their Fate during the Holocaust," *Yad VaShem Studies,* VIII (1970), pp. 31–68. A revised version was published in the author's more comprehensive study in Hebrew, *Sepharad ve-ha-Yehudim bi-yeme ha-Shoah ve-ha-Emancipaziah* [Contemporary Spain and the Jewish People] (Jerusalem, 1975). Based on an analysis of Spanish documents and oral interviews.

Baelman, Franz. "Der Einfluss des Judentums in Griechenland," *Volk im Osten,* IV, 5–6 (1943), pp. 56–62. Nazi propaganda study.

Barzilai, Elias. "Report on the Tragedy of the Jews in Greece," June 14 and 28, 1944. New York, Greek American Council, 1945. The author was the Rabbi of Athens during the war years.

———. "Rescue of the Jews in Athens during the Period of the Nazi Destruction," in *Guinzach Saloniki* (Archives Saloniciennes), Fascicule A, ed. Barouh Ouziel (Tel Aviv, 1961), pp. 90–92 (in Hebrew). English translation prepared by Steven Bowman deposited in Gennadeion Library in Athens, Greece.

Benn, Yoseph. "Sho'ath Yehudei Yavan, 1941–1944" [The Holocaust of the Jews in Greece, 1941–1944] M.A. thesis, University of Tel Aviv, 1977 (unpublished). Author uses Yad VaShem Archives and Zionist Archives; based primarily on Jewish sources available in Israel.

Benveniste, David. *Zikhronoth Ne'urim* [Boyhood Memories] (Jerusalem, 1967).

———. *Yehudei Saloniki be-doroth ha-aharonim* [Thessaloniki Jewry in recent generations] (Jerusalem, 1973). Several chapters detail war years and the holocaust.

Bernard, M. Michael. "Les Israélites de Salonique," rapport preparé par M.

Michael Bernard, Janvier 1913. Dactylographie à New York en 1927 par Henri Basso.

Bowman, Steven. "Remnants and Memories in Greece," *Forum,* 2 (Jerusalem, 1976), pp. 63–71.

———. "The Contribution of Asher Raphael Moisses," *Studies in Bibliography and Booklore,* 12 (Cincinnati, 1979), pp. 25–27. Includes synopsis of career, bibliography of writings, and example from his new demotike translation of Book of Psalms.

———. "Towards a Bibliography of Greek Jewry." Athens, 1973 (typescript). A preliminary listing of some 600 items. A full bibliography on the period after 1500 is in preparation by Robert Attal for the Ben Zvi Institute in Jerusalem.

Centre de documentation juive contemporaine. Musée du memorial du Martyr juif inconnu. Exposition des Juifs dans la lutte contre l'hitlerisme (Paris, n.d.) (1965). Pages 50–54 contain material on Greece and list five Greeks who saved Jews.

Chary, Frederick B. *The Bulgarian Jews and the Final Solution 1940–1944* (Pittsburgh, 1972). Includes chapter on deportations from Thrace and Macedonia.

Cohen, Israel. "The Jews of Greece," *Congress Weekly,* January 25, 1951: 11–12.

Consistoire Central Israélite. Στατιστική [Statistics of Greek Jews] (Athens,1945). Partially published by Joshua Starr in *Jewish Social Studies,*VIII (1945),p. 86.

Contemporary Jewish Record. Review of Events and Digest of Opinions. Volumes IV, V, VI (1941–1943), *passim.*

Czech, Danuta. "Deportation und Vernichtung der griechischen Juden im K.L. Auschwitz," *Hefte von Auschwitz,* 11 (1970), pp. 5–37. Facts and figures on transportation and killing from Auschwitz records.

Dorman, M. *Milhemeth ha-Ezrahim bi-Yavan (Dezember 1944–Yanuar 1945)* [Civil War in Greece, December 1944–January 1945] (Tel Aviv, 1945) (in Hebrew). "EAM was not communist, but rather a league of all anti-royalist factions and groups." Book is an attempt to balance anti-"communist" attitude of Quisling government, Greek monarchy, royalists, fascists, British, and Americans.

Dzelepy, E. *Le drame de la resistance grècque* (Paris, 1946).

Eck, Nathan. "New Light on the Charges Against the Last Grand Rabbi of Salonica," *Yad VaShem Bulletin,* 17 (1965), pp. 9–15 (lacking); complete reprint in ibid., 19 (Oct., 1966), pp. 28–35. Compare document in R. Hilberg, *Documents of Destruction,* pp. 161f. Article is the beginning of the revision of harsh attacks on local leadership.

Elmaleh, Avram. *Les Juifs de Salonique et la Résistance Hellénique* (Istamboul-Salonique, 1949).

Ἡμέρα μνήμης τῶν Ἰσραηλιτῶν Θυμάτων τοῦ Ναζισμοῦ [Memorial Day for the Jewish Victims of Nazism]. Edited by Jewish Community of Athens (Athens,1963).

Emmanuel, Isaac S. *Mazeboth Saloniki* [Precious Stones of the Jews of Thessaloniki] 2 Vols. (Jerusalem, 1963–68). Collection of some 1900 epitaphs dated from 1502–1937. Appendixes include lists of rabbis and teachers killed by Nazis, synagogues and other institutions destroyed, religious academies, various educational, Zionist and religious organizations in pre-war

Thessaloniki; includes a number of photographs documenting the destruction of the graveyard and the reuse of the stones for municipal repairs and for private buildings.

Enepekedes, P.K. Οἱ Διωγμοί τῶν Ἑβραίων ἐν Ἑλλάδι 1941–1944 ἐπί τῇ βάσει τῶν Μυστικῶν Ἀρχείων τῶν ΕΣ-ΕΣ [Die Juden-Verfolgungen in Griechenland 1941–1944. Auf Grund der Geheimakten der SS] (Athens, 1969). A number of vignettes and documents covering many aspects of Holocaust.

Fleischer, Hagen. "Greece Under Axis Occupation, 1941–44: A Bibliographical Survey," *Modern Greek Society: A Social Science Newsletter.* Vol. V, No. 1 (December, 1977), pp. 4–47.

Franco, Hizkia M. *Les Martyrs Juifs de Rhodes et de Cos* (Elizabethville, 1952). Contains lists of victims and survivors.

Friedman, Philip. "The Jews of Greece during the Second World War (A Bibliographical Survey)," *The Joshua Starr Memorial Volume* (New York, 1953), pp. 241–248. Most items supplied by Isaac Kabelli; many written by the latter. Cites a number of ephemera from resistance newspapers and anonymous memoirs.

Gaon, David. *Newspapers in Ladino. A Bibliography* (Jerusalem, 1965) (in Hebrew).

Garlínski, Jósef. *Fighting Auschwitz. The Resistance Movement in the Concentration Camp* (Greenwich, Conn., 1975). Somewhat less detailed than the Polish edition. Author is concerned only with Polish Jews and non-Jews in the resistance and Sonderkommando revolt and ignores presence of Greek Jews.

"Greece," in *American Jewish Yearbook,* Volume 54 (1953), pp. 294–300 by Sam Modiano; vol. 57 (1956), pp. 359–365 by Maurice J. Goldbloom; vol. 61 (1960), pp. 217–222 by Victor Semah.

"Greece," *Encyclopaedia Judaica,* Vol. 7 (Jerusalem, 1971), 875–884. See also under individual cities and *passim.*

"Greece," *The Universal Jewish Encyclopedia,* Vol. 5 (New York, 1941), 91–93. Good survey of modern period by Saul Mézan and Leonard A. Greenberg with emphasis on anti-Jewish measures.

Guinzach Saloniki (Archives Saloniciennes). Ed. Barouh Ouziel. Fascicule A. (Tel Aviv, 1961). Contains several memoirs of interest including that of Rabbi Barzilai.

Gutman, Yisrael and Livia Rothkirchen, eds. *The Catastrophe of European Jewry. Antecedents-History-Reflections.* Selected Papers (Jerusalem, 1976). General background material; quite valuable.

Hilberg, Raul. *The Destruction of European Jews* (Chicago, 1961). Pages 447–452 deal with Greece. Classic statement on passivity of Jews.

———, ed. *Documents of Destruction. Germany and Jewry 1933–1945* (Chicago, 1971). Contains documents on Rabbi Koretz and Mauricius Soriano's Memoir on Rhodes and its Jewish community, pp. 160–171.

Itzhaki, Solomon. "Lights and Shadows in the Balkans," *Congress Weekly,* January 12, 1944: 9–10. Stresses role of the Greeks in helping Jews of Thessaloniki.

Jewish Resistance During the Holocaust. Proceedings of the Conference on Manifestations of Jewish Resistance, Jerusalem, April 7–11, 1968 (Jerusalem, 1971).

"Jews in Greece under Nazi Occupation," *The Ghetto Speaker* (New York, 1944), nos. 22, 25.

Kabelli, Isaac. "The Resistance of the Greek Jews," *YIVO Annual of Jewish Social Sciences*, VIII (1953), pp. 281–288. Much of his material can be verified from other sources but should be used with caution.

Kalinov, Rinah. *Kehilath Saloniki* [The Community of Thessaloniki] (Tel Aviv, 1970).

Kechales, Haim. *Koroth Yehudei Bulgaria* [History of Bulgarian Jewry] Vol. 3. *Bi-tkufath ha-Shoah 1939–1944* (Tel Aviv, 1969). Pages 89–149 deal with the tragedy in Thrace and Macedonia and contain many German and Bulgarian documents. Brief summary of material by author in *Encyclopedia of the Jewish Diaspora*. Volume X. Bulgaria. Edited by Dr. A. Romano, Joseph Ben, et al. (Jerusalem-Tel Aviv, 1969) (in Hebrew).

Kempner, Robert M. *Eichmann und Komplizen* (Zürich, 1961). Contains chapter on Greek Jewry.

Kitsikis, Dimitri. "La famine en Grèce (1941–1942). Les conséquences politiques," *Revue d'Histoire de la Deuxième Guerre Mondiale*, 74 (April, 1969), pp. 17–41.

Lehrman, Hal. "Greece: Unused Cakes of Soap," *Commentary*, Vol. 1, no. 7 (May, 1947), pp. 48–52. Earliest post-war survey by a trained observer, despite seemingly facetious title.

Levi, Primo. *Survival in Auschwitz* (New York, 1961). Contains a poignant impression of the Thessaloniki Jews' presence in Auschwitz written by a sensitive Italian Jew.

Lévy, Jacques B. "Récit de Captivité," *Les Cahiers Séfardis*, I (1947), pp. 178–181, 227–231, 339–345.

Levy, Sam, ed. *Les Cahiers Séfardis*. I–II 1946–1948. Scattered notes on Greek Jews including lists of deportees and survivors.

Matarasso, I. A. . . . Κι' ὅμως ὅλοι τους δὲν πέθαναν . . . Ἡ καταστροφὴ τῶν ἑλληνοεβραίων τῆς Θεσσαλονίκης κατά τήν Γερμανικὴν κατοχήν [And Yet All of Them Did Not Die. The Catastrophe of the Greek Jews of Thessaloniki During the German Occupation] (Athens, 1948). Survey of war years and report on survivors; includes several memoirs.

Matkovsky, Alexander. "The Destruction of Macedonian Jewry," *Yad VaShem* 3 (1959), pp. 222–258. Primarily Yugoslavian Macedonia.

Matsas, Michael N. "How the West Helped Destruction of Greek Jewry," *The Jewish Week*, Washington, D.C., April 13–19, 1978, pp. 48 and 70; correction, April 20–26, 1978, p. 8; rejoinder by Sidney Koretz, May 11–17, 1978, p. 18.

Menasche, Albert. *Birkenau (Auschwitz II). How 72,000 Greek Jews Perished* (New York, 1947). Greek translation, 1974. Eyewitness account by a doctor from Thessaloniki.

Menasché, Bension R. "Les Juifs de Rhodes. Comment ils furent deportées," *Les Cahiers Séfardis*, II (1948), pp. 240–241.

Moisses, Asher. "La situation des communautés juives en Grèce," *Les Juifs en Europe (1939–1945)* (Paris, 1949), pp. 47–54. Post-war summary by communal leader.

———. "Jews in the Army of Greece," in J. Slotsky and M. Kaplan, eds., *Jewish Soldiers in the Armies of Europe* (Tel Aviv, 1967), pp. 182–185; reprinted in *Zikharon Saloniki* (see below) (in Hebrew).

Molho, Henri. "Le judaïsme grec en général et la communauté juive de Salonique en particulier entre les deux guerres mondiales," *Homenage à Millás-Vallierosa,* 2 (Barcelona, 1956), pp. 73–107.

Molho, Isaac. "Documentos para la investigacion mientras la catastrofa hitleriana: Creta-Rhodes, Salonica," *Ozar Yehudei Sepharad* (= Tesoro de los Judios Sefardies), IV (1961), pp. 155–167; V (1962), pp. 152–154 (in Hebrew).

———. "El conte Quinte Mazzolini," ibid., V (1962), pp. 155–157 (in Hebrew). Includes documents in Italian recording efforts on behalf of the Jews of Rhodes.

Molho, Michael. "La nouvelle communauté juive d'Athènes," *The Joshua Starr Memorial Volume* (New York, 1953), pp. 231–239.

Molho, Michael and Joseph Nehama. *In Memoriam. Hommage aux victimes juives des Nazis en Grèce* (Salonique, 1948); reprinted 1975. Revised and expanded version in Hebrew *Shoat Yehudei Yavan 1941–1944* [The Destruction of the Jews of Greece 1941–1944] (Jerusalem, 1965). The latter edition makes use of material in Yad VaShem Archives.

Nehama, Joseph. "Le cimetière juif de Salonique," *Les Cahiers Séfardis,* I (1947), pp. 134–136.

———. "Les bibliothèques juives de Salonique détruites par les Nazis," ibid., pp. 224–226.

———. "Situation actuelle du judaisme en Grèce," ibid., II (1948), pp. 240–241.

Novitch, Miriam. "End of Macedonia and Thrace Jewish Communities," *Ozar Yehudei* Sepharad(=Tesoro de los Judios Sefardies), IV (1961), LIV–LVI.

———. *Gerush Yehudei Saloniki* [Expulsion of the Jews of Thessaloniki], in Dapim le-heker ha-Shoah ve-ha-Mered [Pages towards the study of the Holocaust and the Resistance] (Kibbutz Mordei ha-Ghetta'oth, 1973).

———. *Le passage des barbares; contribution à l'histoire de la deportation et de la résistance des Juifs grecs. Documents inédits et témoignages* (Nice, 197-).

Office nationale hellénique des criminels de guerre. *Les atrocités des quatre envahisseurs de la Grèce: Allemands, Italiens, Bulgares, Albanais.* (Athènes, 1946). "But German crimes against Jews are not included in this study" nor those of the Bulgarians even though 90–97% effective. The execution of Lt. Haim Levy of Yannina is recorded, however.

Pardo, Haim. "Témoinage sur les Juifs à Drama," in Munich-La Dernière Destruction, May, 1948, pp. 88–90 (in Yiddish).

Peikaz, M. et al., eds. *The Jewish Holocaust and Heroism Through the Eyes of the Hebrew Press.* I–IV. (Jerusalem, 1966) (in Hebrew). Extensive bibliography covering all of Palestinian Hebrew Press.

Pohl, J. "Die ehemalige griechische Regierung in ihren Fremdschaftsbetreuerungen gegenüber den Juden," *Die Judenfrage,* no. 16–17 (1942), pp. 177–178. Nazi propaganda study.

———. "Die Zahl der Juden in Griechenland," *Der Weltkampf,* no. 3 (1942), p. 221.

Poliakov, Leon and Jacques Sahille. *The Jews under Italian Occupation* (Paris, 1955): "The Attitudes of the Italians to the Jews in Occupied Greece" by Jacques Sahille, pp. 153–160. Available in French, Italian, and Yiddish.

Politi, M. *Parbarei Atuna* [The Suburbs of Athens] (Tel Aviv, 1966).

Reitlinger, Gerald. *The Final Solution. The Attempt to Exterminate the Jews of Europe 1939–1945* (London, 1968). Greece, pp. 398–408; author stresses passivity.

Roth, Cecil. "The Last Days of Jewish Salonica," *Commentary,* Vol. 10, no. 1 (July, 1950), pp. 49–55.

Sahille, Jacques. "Attitude des Italiens à l'égard des Juifs en Grèce occupée," *Le Monde Juif,* no. 49 (Paris, 1951), pp. 7–10. See above L. Poliakov.

"Salonica," *Encyclopaedia Judaica,* Vol. 14 (Jerusalem, 1971), 669–707.

Saloniki, Ir ve-Em bi-Yisrael [Salonica, A Jewish Metropolis] Edited by the Institute for the Study of Salonican Jewry (Jerusalem-Tel Aviv, 1967). Memorial volume containing a number of articles and memoirs.

Sciaky, Leon. *Farewell to Salonica: Portrait of an Era* (New York, 1946).

Shiby, Barukh, ed. *Haggadah shel Pessach* (Thessaloniki, 1971). Contains a detailed map of pre-war Jewish Thessaloniki, pp. 120–125.

Sporiades, G. "'Ο μεγάλος διωγμός. Τό ξεκλήρισμα τῶν 'Ελλήνων 'Εβραίων" (The Great Persecution. The Extermination of the Greek Jews), *Ethnos,* 17. 1–2.3.55.

Starr, Joshua. "The Socialist Federation of Saloniki," *Jewish Social Studies,* VII (1945), pp. 323–336.

Stavrianos, L.S. "The Jews of Greece," *Journal of Central European Affairs,* VIII (October, 1948), pp. 256–269. Valuable early survey including post-war problems.

Steckel, Charles W. *Destruction and Survival* (Los Angeles, 1973). Yugoslavian story including documents by local rabbi; contains valuable critique of Holocaust historiography.

Steinberg, Lucien. "Greek Jews in the Battle against Nazism," in M. Mushkat, ed., *Jews in the Allied Forces in the Fight Against Nazism* (Merhaviah, 1971), pp. 327–331 (in Hebrew).

"The Jewish Remnant in Greece," *Congress Weekly,* September 17, 1948: 14.

The Jews and The Liberation Struggle: a report of the Central Committee of EAM on the Jews of Greece and the Liberation Struggle (n.p., n.d.) [1945?].

The Jews in Greece. New York, American Jewish Committee, June, 1944.

The Massacre of a People. New York, Jewish Frontier Association, 1944.

Tsatsos, Jeanne. *The Sword's Fierce Edge. A Journal of the Occupation of Greece, 1941–1944.* Tr. Jean Demos (Nashville: Vanderbilt University Press, 1969). Records efforts of Archbishop Damaskinos to rescue Jews.

Vasileva, Nadeja Slavi. "On the Catastrophe of the Thracian Jews: Recollection," *Yad VaShem,* 3(1959), pp. 295–302.

Vogel, Georg. *Diplomat unter Hitler und Adenauer* (Düsseldorf: Econ, 1969). Pages 94ff describe deportation of Athenian Jews.

World Jewish Congress. Advisory Council on European Jewish Affairs. Reports on the Jewish Situation. *The Situation of the Jews in Greece* (New York, 1944).

Yaacovi, Yohanan. "The Road to Captivity. A Short History of the Palestinian units which served in the campaigns of Greece and Crete in the Spring of

1941." M.A. thesis. University of Tel Aviv, 1976 (unpublished; text in Hebrew with English summary).

Yacoel, Yom Tov. *Yoman [Diary] (Jerusalem, 1961).*

Yad VaShem. *Saloniki, Koroth Ir ve-Em bi-Yisrael* [Saloniki, Story of a Jewish Metropolis]. Edited by Yehuda Arni and Peretz Alufi (Jerusalem, 1975).

Zevgadakis, Nik. E. "Οἱ 'Εβραίοι τῆς Κρήτης κατά τήν Γερμανικὴν Κατοχήν" [The Jews of Crete during the German Occupation], Μεσόγειος [Cretan Daily Newspaper], 4 September 1963.

Zikharon Saloniki, Gedulateh ve-Ḥorbanah shel Yerushalayim de-Balkan [Memorial for Thessaloniki, Grandeur and Destruction of the Jerusalem of the Balkans]. Edited by David Recanati. Vol. 1 (Tel Aviv, 1972) (in Hebrew). Memorial book containing articles and memoirs including a history of the Jews in Thessaloniki by I. S. Emmanuel.

Contributors

STEVEN BOWMAN received his graduate training at the Hebrew University in Jerusalem and at Ohio State University. He taught Jewish history at Indiana University (1974–1976) and was a visiting professor at the University of California (Berkeley and San Diego), the University of Massachusetts, and Haifa University. Recently he joined the Program of Judaic Studies of the University of Cincinnati. His primary research is on the Jews of the Byzantine Empire, and he has written a number of articles on the Jews in medieval and modern Greece.

HAGEN FLEISCHER received his doctorate degree in history and mass media science from the Free University of Berlin. He is research associate of the Center for the Study of Modern Greek History of the Academy of Athens and guest lecturer on European history at the University of Athens. He is the author of various articles on wartime Greece and of a forthcoming book, "Greece, 1941–1944. A Political History."

JOHN O. IATRIDES received his education in Greece, the Netherlands, and the United States (Ph.D. Clark University, 1962). He served with the Greek National Defense General Staff (1955–1956) and the Prime Minister's Press Office (1956–1958), and is now professor of international politics at Southern Connecticut State College. He has taught courses on contemporary Greece at Yale and Harvard universities. His principal publications include *Balkan Triangle, Birth and Decline of an Alliance Across Ideological Boundaries* (1968), *Revolt in Athens. The Greek Communist "Second Round," 1944–1945* (1972), *Ambassador MacVeagh Reports. Greece, 1933–1947* (1980), and has edited *Greek-American Relations. A Critical Review* (1980, with Theodore A. Couloumbis), and *Greece in the 1940s. A Nation in Crisis* (1981). He is book review editor for *Balkan Studies* (Thessaloniki) and also edits the semi-annual *Bulletin* of the Modern Greek Studies Association.

Library of Congress Cataloging in Publication Data

Fleischer, Hagen.
Greece in the 1940s.

Companion to: Greece in the 1940s : a nation in crisis.
1. Greece—History—Bibliography.
I. Iatrides, John O. II. Bowman, Steven.
III. Greece in the 1940s : a nation in crisis.
IV. Title.
Z2296.F56 [DF757] 016.9495'074 80-54473
ISBN 0-87451-199-2 (pbk.) AACR2